Getting Your Affairs in Order:

AN OWNER'S MANUAL

L. John Hartmann
CEO and President

This document discusses general concepts for retirement planning, and is not intended to provide tax or legal advice. Individuals are urged to consult with their tax and legal professionals regarding these issues. This handbook should ensure that clients understand a) that annuities and some of their features have costs associated with them; b) that income received from annuities is taxable; and c) that annuities used to fund IRAs do not afford any additional measure of tax deferral for the IRA owner.

Printed in the United States of America

First Printing, 2014

Gradient Positioning Systems, LLC
4105 Lexington Avenue North, Suite 110
Arden Hills, MN 55126 (877) 901-0894

Gradient Positioning Systems, LLC and L. John Hartmann are not affiliated with or endorsed by the Social Security Administration or any government agency.

Acknowledgements

I would like to give credit to the following people because without their contributions this book would not have been possible: to my wife Helen, who always held down the home front while I was on the road assisting clients; to my sister Mary Nelson and my nephew Mike Nelson, who helped provide ideas for the graphics; to the people at Gradient Financial Group, LLC, namely Brooke Tucker, Ben Seitz, Brian Gragert, and their assisting personnel, who supported my efforts while I was in the field; and finally, to Nick Stovall, Mike Binger, Nate Lucius, and Gradient Positioning Systems, LLC, who helped bring everything together.

Table of Contents

Introduction

The rigors of everyday living often feel like occupation enough: from paying bills to filling the gas tank to making dinner, the number of items on a day's to-do list can easily be greater than the 24-hours within it. The demands placed on our time and finances often make it difficult to successfully manage the logistics of our immediate futures, nonetheless our distant ones. While this is an entirely familiar and understandable predicament, it is a quandary that can have far-reaching implications, especially when it comes to getting their affairs in order to prepare for their retirement and for the transfer of their assets to their beneficiaries. All too often, people delay getting their affairs in order for such a long time that when they finally do begin the process they may no longer have the luxury of flexibility that a longer time frame would have afforded them. By taking the time to develop a plan today, you can preserve tomorrow's future for yourself and, most importantly, for your loved ones.

Most of us have spent our entire adult lives working and saving money. As you approach retirement, perhaps you have become aware of how much you would like your saved assets to be able to accomplish: they need to be used for income, accumulation, long-term healthcare, and planning your legacy. Moreover, your assets need to be able to perform these functions without leaving you vulnerable to undue risk because this is not a time in your life when you can afford to gamble with your future. Successfully accommodating all those expectations will be no small feat, especially when you take the current turbulence of our economy into account: between low interest rates, the constant yo-yoing of inflation, an uncertain tax landscape and intense market volatility, the demands of this situation are unusually diverse and the stakes are undeniably high.

In other words, getting your affairs in order is often a daunting jumble of investment ideas and asset allocation strategies that are difficult to unify or execute. Ultimately, the only way to effectively complete this journey is by utilizing a central coordinator who understands the various financial, legal and logistical components and can help you develop a purposeful, coordinated and cohesive plan to address your future financial needs. Trying to plan for your retirement and organize your estate is like having a ship with three rudders: it's impossible to make progress without someone developing and coordinating a plan. To this end, the success of your retirement and the clarity of the organization of your estate is much more likely to be achieved if you work with a financial professional who can provide oversight, coordination and direction. The purpose of this book is not to supply you with a step-by-step guide to retirement and the organization of your estate. Rather, this book is meant to arm you with the tools and questions you need to begin securing you and your family's future comfort and needs.

You have spent a lifetime working for your money and this is now the point in your life where it goes to work for you. You want to develop a plan that will leverage your assets enough so they will be capable of generating an income, but not at the expense of their preservation. Solving this problem is what all plans for retirement seek to address. However, most plans focus solely on retirement and then include a few hasty provisions meant to help with legacy planning. Getting your affairs in order, however, is about using a comprehensive and coordinated financial approach utilizing an estate planner. In other words, enlisting the assistance of a financial professional will help you develop a plan to put your money to work during your retirement and legacy, but it will also do so in the least expensive, most expeditious and tax avoidant way. Essentially, you are looking for strategies that will protect the assets you have already accumulated by developing a plan to safely structure them for retirement income and sheltering them so that your beneficiaries will quickly be able to access them.

There are many different financial vehicles and strategies that can be employed to accomplish these goals. By examining your personal and financial goals and using this book as a general guide, an outline for the ordering of your affairs may become discernible.

1
Organizing Your Assets

Will we have enough money for retirement?

Lizzie and Alex have always put planning for their retirement on hold in favor of focusing on more immediate matters. However, with their 61st birthdays looming on the horizon, Lizzie and Alex have suddenly become aware that it's time to have a real plan for their future in place. They know they will each be able to rely on Social Security benefits and that the earliest they can file for them is when they turn 62, but they're not sure how much their monthly checks would be if they filed then or if that would even be the most advantageous time for them to file.

Besides their Social Security benefit, Lizzie also has a 401(k) through her employer but she doesn't really know how it works, how she can begin drawing money from it, or how much income it will provide once she retires. Additionally, she knows other retirement ac-

count options exist but she doesn't know if she should switch to one of them or, if she should, which one would best fit her family's needs. Alex, on the other hand, will be able to start collecting his pension at age 67 but, if they can afford it, he'd like to retire before then. Finally, the couple just celebrated the birth of their first grandchild so whatever retirement plan they develop, they would like it to include preparations for the organization of their estate, as well, so they know their family will be taken care of after they're gone. But where to begin?

While Lizzie and Alex may sound like they're totally in the dark about their retirement, the truth is there are a lot of people just like them. Perhaps you are even one of them. While you may have built up a 401(k), an IRA, and Social Security benefits, do you know what your financial picture really looks like?

If you don't have a precise answer to that question, you're in good company. Many people know retirement is coming and that they will have some assets to rely on, but they aren't sure how it will all come together to provide them with a retirement income. Far too often, people spend their entire working lives hoping what they put into their retirement accounts will help them live comfortably once they clock out of the workforce for good. While hoping for the best is an understandable sentiment, it can make the idea of retirement feel like an ominously unavoidable problem rather than a rewarding life stage.

Preparing for retirement is unlike any fiscal challenge you have ever faced before: not only does it require a complete remodeling of your financial house but in order to do so, you must use an entirely new financial perspective and toolset. Prior to retiring, your finances are predicated on an earning and saving financial model: you go to work, earn money, and save some of it for the future. Once you retire, you will no longer be going to work and drawing a paycheck so those familiar financial rules become moot. Of course, your need for money won't end just because your career has, so you will need to have a plan in place that replaces your old working paycheck with an income created from your existing assets. In other words, you will need to shift from an earning and saving paradigm to an income and asset leveraging paradigm where you use the money you have earned and saved to generate income and preserve your assets for you.

Structuring assets to create an income-generating retirement requires a different approach than earning income via the workforce. Saving money for retirement, which is what you have spent your life doing, and *planning* your retirement are two different things. Both are important. Earning and saving money is different than creating a financial strategy that will position your assets in a way that will preserve them but also capitalize upon them so your income needs in retirement will be satisfied. This is no easy task.

When you consider the complexities of taxes, the logistics of required minimum distributions (RMDs) from IRAs, and the oft-overlooked importance of legacy planning, you can begin to see why happy endings require more than hope. They require a focused and well-executed plan.

In regard to retirement, your financial life can be thought of as consisting of three main phases: contribution, distribution, and transfer. The contribution phase is the one you spend most of your life in: it lasts as long as you are still working and saving money for your retirement. The distribution phase begins when you reach the point of relying on your assets for income. Finally, the transfer stage is how your assets will be passed on to your loved ones after you are gone. For now, we will focus on the distribution phase, the point at which you will need to begin drawing income from your retirement assets. ***Every financial strategy for retirement needs first to accommodate the day-to-day need for income.***

Entry into the distribution phase of your plan is sometimes referred to as jumping off the **retirement cliff** because the transition from relying on your salary to your assets to provide you with income can be abrupt without proper planning. Leaving your retirement up to chance is unadvisable by nearly any standard, yet millions of people find themselves *hoping* instead of planning for a soft landing. You don't have to be one of them. With information, tools and professional guidance, you can create a successful retirement plan that will put you in control of your financial management.

Now that you know there's more to saving and planning for retirement than filing for your Social Security benefit and drawing income from your 401(k), you can begin to **create a strategy for your retirement** that can have a significant impact on your financial landscape after you stop drawing a paycheck. Understanding how to manage your assets entails risk management, risk diversification, tax planning and income planning preparation throughout your life stages. These strategies can help you leverage more from each one of the hard-earned dollars you set aside for your retirement.

Some people file for Social Security on day one of their retirement. Others rely on supplemental income from an IRA or another retirement account. Working with a financial professional can help you determine your best course of action.

NEW IDEAS FOR A NEW WORLD

The transition from the contribution phase to the distribution phase of your retirement plan must be accompanied by a concurrent shift in the financial perspective you use to frame the organization of your assets. However, preparing for this conversion is not the only change your plan needs to account for. The reality is that investment strategies and savings plans that used to be thought of as being capable of withstanding the test of time may no longer be applicable because they have encountered challenging new circumstances that have turned them on their heads.

Our world is in a constant state of flux and the financial strategy you select must be capable of adapting to changing conditions in the market and the economy at large, as well as to changes in your personal circumstances.

In the early 1990s, investing in the market or in financial products such as CDs or bonds would both yield similar rates of return because this period was characterized by high interest rates and low market volatility. Basically, the low market volatility meant investors could take advantage of the market's growth potential without exposing their investments to undue risk, while the high interest rates meant investors also had the option of avoiding the uncertainty of the market altogether because they could invest their money in safer financial products and it could still comfortably accumulate. At that time, you had the option of exposing yourself to both an acceptable amount of risk and an acceptable fixed interest rate, which meant you were likely to be fairly successful with a wide range of investment options. In other words, it was difficult to make a mistake during that time period.

Today, you don't have those options. Market volatility is at an all-time high while interest rates are at all-time lows. They are so far apart from each other that it is hard to know what to do with your money. Yesterday's investment rules may not work today. Not only could they hamper achieving your goals, they may actually harm your financial situation. We are currently in a period when interest rates are at historic lows, and the volatility of the market is higher than ever. There is no overlapping acceptable rate, making both options less than ideal. *Because of this uncertain financial landscape, wise investment strategies are now more important than ever.*

This unique situation requires fresh ideas and investment tools that haven't been relied on in the past. Investing the way your parents did will not pay off. The majority of investment ideas used by financial professionals in the 1990s aren't applicable in today's

|

markets. That kind of investing will likely get you in trouble and compromise your retirement. For example, the Great Recession of the early 2000's highlighted how old investment ideas were not only ineffective but incredibly destructive to the retirement plans of millions of Americans. The dawn of an entirely restructured health care system brings with it new options and challenges that will undoubtedly change the way insurance companies provide investment products and services. Longer life expectancies and increasing healthcare concerns means having a long-term care strategy in place for the end of your life needs to be a primary focus instead of an afterthought.

Perhaps the most important lessons investors learned from the Great Recession is that not understanding where your money is invested (and the potential risks of those investments) can work against you, your plans for retirement and your legacy. Saving and investing money isn't enough to truly get the most out of it. You must have a planful approach to managing your assets.

Essentially, managing your money and your investments is an ongoing process that requires customization and adaptation to a changing world. And make no mistake; the world is always changing. What worked for your parents or even your parents' parents was probably good advice back then. People in retirement or approaching retirement today need new ideas and professional guidance. Today, you need a better PLAN.

HOPE SO VS. KNOW SO MONEY

Now that you have a better idea of the general outline of the financial picture you're facing, let's take a closer look at the money that gives it color.

There are essentially two kinds of money: *Hope So* and *Know So*. Everyone can divide their money into these two categories. Some have more of one kind than the other. The goal isn't to eliminate one kind of money but to balance them as you approach retirement.

Hope So Money, as the name implies, is money that you hope will be there when you need it in the future. It is money that fluctuates with the market, which means it is exposed to more risk but also has the potential for more reward. However, Hope So Money has no minimum guarantee and is subject to a variety of factors, such as investor activity, stock prices, market trends, and buying trends, which means you can't really be sure what the value of your investments will be worth in the future. In other words, because this money relies on the market and the market is

10-Year Treasury Long-term Fixed Rates

Volatility Index – or *Fear Gauge:* Implied Market Volatility

Source: Yahoo Finance – 12-31-2013. VIX is a trademarked ticker symbol for the Chicago Board Options Exchange Market Volatility Index, a popular measure of the implied volatility of S&P 500 index options. Often referred to as the fear index or the fear gauge, it represents one measure of the market's expectation of stock market volatility over the next 30 day period (wikipedia.com). The CBOE 10-year Treasury Note (TNX) is based on 10 times the yield-to-maturity on the most recently auctioned 10-year Treasury note. Past performance does not guarantee future results. Some illustrations may show how a market index has performed. An investor cannot invest in an index, although there are some investments designed to mirror index performance. Past performance is not a guarantee of future results.

The VIX, or volatility index, of the market represents expected market volatility. When the VIX drops, economic experts expect less volatility. When the VIX rises, more volatility is expected.

1. *VIX is a trademarked ticker symbol for the Chicago Board Options Exchange (CBOE) Market Volatility Index, a popular measure of the implied volatility of S&P 500 index options. Often referred to as the fear index or the fear gauge, it represents one measure of the market's expectation of stock market volatility over the next 30 day period. (wikipedia.com)*
2. *The CBOE 10-Year Treasury Note (TNX) is based on 10 times the yield-to-maturity on the most recently auctioned 10-year Treasury note.*

subject to change, you can't rely on Hope So Money. This doesn't mean you shouldn't have some money invested in the market, but it would be dangerous to assume you can know what it will be worth in the future. This is why we call it Hope So Money: because it represents the amount you would like to get out of your investments.

Hope So Money is an important element of a retirement plan, especially in the early stages of planning when a longer investment timeframe is available to you, which means you can trade volatility for potential returns. In the long run, time can smooth out the ups and downs of money exposed to the market. Working with a professional and leveraging a long-term investment strategy has the potential to create rewarding returns from Hope So Money. Frequently encountered types of Hope So Money include:

- Stock market funds, including index funds
- Mutual funds
- Variable annuities
- REITs

Know So Money, by contrast, is money you can count on. It is made up of dependable, low-risk to no-risk investments that you can be fairly certain will be there when you need it in the future. While this money is not exposed to the same levels of market volatility as Hope So Money, this also means it does not bear a similar potential for returns.

One of the most common types of Know So Money is Social Security. Income you draw or will draw from Social Security is guaranteed. You have paid into Social Security your entire career, and you can rely on that money during your retirement. Unlike the market, rates of growth for Know So Money are dependent on 10-year treasury rates. The 10-year treasury, or TNX, is commonly considered to represent a very secure and safe place for your money. The 10-year treasury drives key rates for things such as mortgage rates or CD rates. Know So Money may not be as exciting as Hope So Money, but it is safer. In addition to Social Security, some other common examples of Know So Money include:

- Government backed bonds
- Savings and checking accounts
- Fixed income annuities
- CDs
- Treasuries
- Money market accounts

Knowing the difference between Hope So and Know So Money is an important step towards a successful retirement plan. People who are 55 or older and who are looking ahead to retirement should be relying on more Know So Money than Hope So Money.

Ideally, the rates of return on Hope So and Know So Money would have an overlapping area that provided an acceptable rate of risk for both types of money. However, as mentioned earlier, these rates are currently at opposite ends of the spectrum: market volatility is at an all-time high, while interest rates are at historic lows. As a result, in order for a retirement plan to be successful it must incorporate a healthy balance of both Hope So and Know So Money. Too much of either kind of money will cause your plan to fail: if it relies too heavily on Hope So Money, it will be exposed to high amounts of risk, which means any market downturn would have catastrophic implications on your assets and you could lose some, if not all, of your retirement money. On the other hand, if your plan is overly dependent on Know So Money, your investments would actually end up decreasing in value because the current interest rates barely keep pace with inflation.

The average investor needs to accumulate enough assets to create a retirement plan that will accommodate their day-to-day income needs during retirement and also allow for legacy planning. To accomplish this, you have to balance the level of risk your assets are exposed to by having a reasonable amount of both Hope So and Know So Money.

> » *Ali has maintained a small brokerage account that he invests in whenever he can. A couple years ago, he changed jobs and decided it was time to transfer his 401(k) assets into an IRA so he could take advantage of a larger selection of investment options. Now, at age 59, he is a few years away from retirement and beginning to more actively plan for the next stage of his life. In doing so, he has suddenly become aware that practically every dollar he has saved for retirement is tied up in the market and therefore subject to risk. He knows he needs to begin to shift some of his assets into a safer investment vehicle that is less exposed to market volatility but he wants some of his money to still provide a decent potential for growth. How can he decide how much money to keep in the market and how much to set aside?*

Ali's predicament is not unusual. Many investors don't know how vulnerable to risk their assets are. Organizing your assets by making a list of all your financial holdings is a helpful way to develop a clearer understanding of how much of your money is at risk and how much is in safer holdings. But how much Know So Money is enough to secure your income needs during retirement, and how much Hope So Money is enough to allow you to continue to benefit from an improving market? Moreover, how much money do you need to maintain your lifestyle and when do you need it? In short, how do you begin to know how much risk you should be exposed to?

Answering this question is at the crux of developing a sustainable retirement plan.

RULE OF 100

Determining the amount of risk that is right for you is dependent on a number of variables. Everyone's risk diversification will be different depending on the unique parameters set by their particular circumstances. Your age, health, comfort level, and financial situation are just a few of the factors that will help to determine the level of risk to which your assets should be exposed. You need to feel comfortable with where and how you are investing your money, and your financial professional is obligated to help you make decisions that put your money in places that fit within your risk criteria. While there is no single approach to investment risk determination advice that is universally applicable to everyone, there are some helpful guidelines.

The Rule of 100 is a general rule that helps shape asset diversification* for the average investor. The rule states that the number 100 minus an investor's age equals the amount of assets they should have exposed to risk.

The Rule of 100: 100 - (your age) = the percentage of your assets that should be exposed to risk (Hope So Money)

For example, if you are a 30-year-old investor, the Rule of 100 would indicate that you should be focusing on investing primarily in the market and taking on a substantial amount of risk in your portfolio. The Rule of 100 suggests that 70 percent of your investments should be exposed to risk.

100 - (30 years of age) = 70 percent

Asset Diversification disclosure – Diversification and asset allocation does not assure of guarantee better performance and cannot eliminate the risk of investment loss. Before investing, you should carefully read the applicable volatility disclosure for each of the underlying funds, which can be found in the current prospectus.

As this example illustrates, according to the Rule of 100 risk tolerance generally decreases as you get older. This is because much of the flexibility that comes from investing earlier in life has to do with *compounding.* Compounded earnings can be incredibly powerful over time. The longer amount of time your money has to compound, the greater your wealth will be. This is what most people talk about when they refer to putting their money to work. This is also why the Rule of 100 favors risk for the young. If you start investing when you are young, you can invest smaller amounts of money in a more aggressive fashion because you have the potential to make a profit in a rising market and you can harness the power of compounding earnings. When you are 40, 50 or 60 years old, that potential becomes less and less and you are forced to have more money at lower amounts of risk to realize the same returns. **It basically becomes more expensive to prudently invest the older you get.**

As you age, the amount of time your money will have to recover becomes shorter, so you should have less of your assets in volatile investments where they will be exposed to more risk. By using the Rule of 100 as a guide, it becomes easier to determine how many of your assets you should shift to safer holdings to ensure that they will still be there when you need to rely on them to provide you with income during your retirement.

Perhaps when you were age 30 and starting your career, like in the example above, it made sense to have 70 percent of your

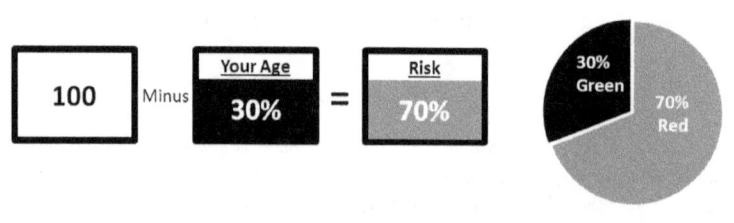

money in the market: you had time on your side. You had plenty of time to save more money, work more and recover from a downturn in the market. Retirement was ages away, and your earning power was increasing. And indeed, younger investors should take on more risk for exactly those reasons. The potential reward of long-term involvement in the market outweighs the risk of investing when you are young.

Likewise, if you are 40 years old and lose 30 percent of your portfolio in a market downturn this year, you have 20 or 30 years to recover it. If you are 68 years old, you have five to 10 years (or less) to make the same recovery. That new circumstance changes your whole retirement perspective. At age 68, it's likely that you simply aren't as interested in suffering through a tough stock market. There is less time to recover from downturns, and the stakes are higher. The money you have saved is money you will soon need to provide you with income, or is money that you already need to meet your income demands.

Let's look at one more example that illustrates how the Rule of 100 becomes more critical as you age. An 80-year-old investor who is retired and is relying on retirement assets for income needs to depend on a solid amount of Know So Money. The Rule of 100 says an 80-year-old investor should have a maximum of 20 percent of his or her assets at risk. Depending on the investor's financial position, even less risk exposure may be required. You are the only person who can make this kind of determination, but the Rule of 100 can help. Everyone has their own level of comfort. Your Rule of 100 results will be based on your values and attitudes as well as your comfort with risk.

Of course, your ability to bear risk is dependent on more than your age. For instance, not every 30-year-old should have exactly 70 percent of their assets in mutual funds and stocks. The Rule of 100 is based on your chronological age, not your "financial age," which could vary based on your investment experience, your aversion or acceptance of risk and a variety of other factors. While this rule isn't an ironclad solution to anyone's finances, it's a pretty good place to start. Once you've taken the time to look at your assets with a professional to determine your risk exposure, you can use the Rule of 100 to make changes that put you in a more stable investment position — one that reflects your comfort level.

Additionally, the Rule of 100 can apply to overarching financial management and to specific investment products that you own as well. Take the 401(k) for example. Many people have them, but not many people understand how their money is allocated within their 401(k). An employer may have someone who comes in once a year and explains the models and options that employees can choose from, but that's as much guidance as most 401(k) holders get. Many 401(k) options include target date funds that change their risk exposure over time, essentially following a form of the Rule of 100. Selecting one of these options can often be a good move for employees because they shift your risk as you age, securing more Know So Money when you need it.

A financial professional can look at your assets with you and discuss alternatives to optimize your balance between Know So and Hope So Money.

CHAPTER 1 RECAP //

- There is money you hope you'll have in the future, and there's money you know you'll have in the future. Make sure you know how much you need when you retire.
- Organizing your assets starts with making a list. You can then understand how each asset is balanced for risk.
- Your exposure to risk is ultimately determined by you.
- Use the Rule of 100 as a general guiding principle when determining how much risk your retirement investments should be exposed to (100 - [your age] = [percentage of your investments that can comfortably exposed to risk]).

2

The Color of Money

As we have seen, it's more important than ever to know where your money is, where you would like it to be, and to develop a plan that will help to get it there. The unfortunate truth of the situation is that many people don't have a clear understanding of their finances, which means they don't know their level of exposure to risk nor do they have a truly viable strategy to protect or accumulate their assets. In today's world, it's more important than ever to know which of your assets are at risk. High market volatility and low treasury rates make for challenging financial topography. Navigating this financial landscape starts with planful asset management that takes into account your specific needs and options.

Visually organizing your assets is an important and powerful way to get a clear picture of what kind of money you have, where it is and how you can best use it in the future. This process is as simple as listing your assets and assigning them a color based on their status as Know So or Hope So Money.

It can be helpful to assign colors to the different kinds of money and their level of risk. For our purposes, Know So Money (which is safer and more dependable) is green. Hope So Money (which is exposed to risk and fluctuates with the market) is red. A financial professional can help you better understand the color of the money in your investment portfolio. Work with your financial professional to create a comprehensive inventory of your assets to understand what you are working with before making any decisions. This may be the first time you have ever sat down and sorted out all of your assets, allowing you to see how much money you have at risk in the market. Comparing the color of your investments will give you an idea of how near or far you are from adhering to the Rule of 100.

Over the course of your lifetime, it is likely that you have acquired a variety of assets. Assets can range from money that you have in a savings account or a 401(k), to a pension or an IRA. You have earned money and have made financial decisions based on the best information you had at the time. When viewed as a whole, however, you might not have an overall strategy for the management of your assets.

Green Money	Red Money
"Green Money" is safer.	"Red Money" is at risk.
This is money that offers a minimum guarantee but it may pose risks other than market risk.	This is money that can go up or down in value. It may pose risk if it is not properly managed to serve a specific purpose in a comprehensive plan.

Even if you feel that you have plenty of money in your 401(k) or IRA, not knowing how much *risk* those investments are exposed to can cause you major financial suffering. Take the market crash of 2008 for example. In 2008, the average investor lost 30 percent of their 401(k). If more people had shifted their investments away from risk as they neared retirement age (i.e. the Rule of 100), they may have lost a lot less money going into retirement.

However, as you learned in the previous chapter, when you use the Rule of 100 to calculate your level of risk, you might discover your financial age is different than your chronological age. The way you organize your assets depends on your goals and your level of comfort with risk. Whatever you determine the appropriate amount of risk for you to be, you will need to organize your portfolio to reflect your goals. If you have more Red Money than Green Money, in particular, you will need to make decisions about how to move it. You can work with a financial professional to find appropriate Green Money options for your situation. As you organize your assets and begin to more closely examine your Green Money, you might realize that it's not all the same shade of green. In fact, depending on when you need to rely on it, there are actually two types of Green Money: Need Now Money and Need Later Money.

IT'S NOT EASY BEING GREEN: NEED NOW MONEY AND NEED LATER MONEY

Considering that the success of your retirement plan hinges upon its capacity to provide you with a lifetime supply of income, you will need to have a healthy abundance of Green Money so you can be confident in the fact that you will have the income you need when you need it. As you know, one of the most critical components of your plan is that it must be able to satisfy your daily income need and it must be able to do so beginning on day one of your retirement. This is your Need Now Money. It's the money you will use for immediate income so you can meet your basic needs, pay your bills, your mortgage (if you have one), and any other costs associated with maintaining your lifestyle.

However, because you will also need income on day 3,650 of your retirement, you will want to invest some of your money so it can grow and be used to meet your income needs in five, 10, or 20 years. The money used for accumulation is Need Later Money: it's money that you don't need for income right now, but you will need it for income down the road. It's still Green Money because you will rely on it later for income and will need to count on it being there. Need Later Money represents income your assets will need to generate for future use.

When planning your retirement, it is vital to decide how much of your assets to structure for income and how much to set aside to accumulate to create Need Later Money. You must figure out if your income and accumulation needs are met. Your Need Now and Need Later Money are top priorities. Need Now Money, in particular, will dictate what your options for future needs are.

As we saw with the Rule of 100, low-risk investments, Green Money, in other words, becomes much more important as you age. While you want to reduce the amount of Red Money you have and to transition it to Green Money, you don't necessarily need all of it to generate income for you right away. Applying the Rule of 100 is one way you can begin to decide how you want to calibrate the scale between your Red and Green Money. Investing heavily in Red Money and gambling all of your assets on the market is incredibly risky no matter where you fall within the Rule of 100. Money in the market can't be depended on to generate income, and a plan that leans too heavily on Red Money can easily fail, especially when investment decisions are influenced by emotional reactions to market downturns and recoveries. Not only is this an unwise plan, it can be incredibly stressful to an investor who is gambling everything on stocks and mutual funds.

But a plan that uses too much Green Money avoids all volatility and can also fail. Why? Investing all of your money in Certificates of Deposit (CDs), savings accounts, money markets and other low return accounts may provide interest and income, but that likely won't be enough to keep pace with inflation. If you focus exclusively on income from Green Money and avoid owning any stocks or mutual funds in your portfolio, you won't be able to leverage the potential for long-term growth your portfolio needs to stay healthy and productive. This is where the Rule of 100 can help you determine how much of your money should be invested in the market to anticipate your future needs.

For your retirement plan to be successful, it must satisfy your daily need for income in a sustainable manner so that you can be assured you will always have the money you need, regardless of whether you need it on day 3 of retirement or day 5,000 of retirement. In other words, your plan must effectively play the short and long game, which means your assets have to be structured so they are able to both accumulate and provide income, but not in a way that overly-antagonizes your risk tolerance. Accomplishing this goal will require a blend of both Red and Green Money. Determining the appropriate ratio between the two will depend on your circumstance, personal preference, and, of course, knowing how much money you need by creating an income plan.

A NUMBERS GAME: CREATING AN INCOME PLAN

Evaluating your income needs will help you find the most efficient and beneficial way to address them, which will have impacts on your lifestyle, your asset accumulation and your legacy planning after you retire. When you have identified your income need, you will know how much to structure for income and how much to be set aside for accumulation. This is where your Green Money comes into play: the safer, more reliable assets that you have accumulated that can be designed to provide you with a steady income.

Always remember that on day one of your retirement, you will need a steady and reliable supply of income from your Green Money. Satisfying that need for daily income entails first knowing *how much you need* and *when you will need it.*

How Much Money Do You Need? While this amount will be different for everyone, the general rule of thumb is that a retiree will require 70 to 80 percent of their pre-retirement income to maintain their lifestyle. Once you know what that number is, the key becomes matching your income need with the correct investment strategies, options and tools to satisfy that need.

When Do You Need Your Money? If you need income to last 10 years, use a tool that creates just that. If you need a lifetime of income, seek a tool that will do that and won't run out.

So how do you figure out how much you need and when you need it? When you take health care costs, potential emergencies, plans for moving or traveling, and other retirement expenses into account, you can really give your calculator a workout. You want to maximize retirement benefits to meet your lifetime income needs. An Investment Advisor can help you answer those questions by working with you to customize an income plan. As you create your income plan, keep in mind that the main goal is not to figure out how to find more money, but to utilize the money you already have in the most effectively profitable way so it can generate the income you need.

As we determined earlier in Chapter 1, the most important thing you need to do as you create an income plan is to take care to avoid too much exposure to risk. You can start by meeting with an Investment Advisor to organize your assets. Get your Green Money and Red Money in order and balanced to meet your needs. If the market goes down 18 percent this afternoon, you don't want that to come out of what you're relying on for next year's income.

OPTIMIZING RISK AND FINDING THE RIGHT BALANCE

Determining the amount of risk that is right for you depends on your specific situation and it starts by using the Rule of 100 to dissect your particular financial position to discover what the right amount of risk is for you.

Remember that the Rule of 100 is just a baseline. Use it as a starting point for figuring out where your money should be. If you're a 50-year-old investor, the Rule of 100 suggests that you have 50 percent Green Money and 50 percent Red Money. Most 50-year-olds are more risk tolerant, however. There are many reasons why someone might be more risk tolerant, not the least of which is feeling young! Experienced investors, people who feel they need to gamble for a higher return, or people who have met their retirement income goals and are looking for additional ways to accumulate wealth are all candidates for investment strategies that incorporate higher levels of risk. In the end, it comes down to your personal tolerance for risk. How much are you willing to lose?

Consulting with a financial professional is often the wisest approach to calculating your risk level. A professional can help determine your risk tolerance by getting to know you, asking you a set of questions and even giving you a survey to determine your comfort level with different types of risk. Here's a typical scenario a financial professional might pose to you:

"You have $100,000 saved that you would like to invest in the market. There is an investment product that could turn your $100,000 into $120,000. That same option, however, has the potential of losing you up to $30,000, leaving you with $70,000."

Is that a scenario that you are willing to enter into? Or are you more comfortable with this one:

"You could turn your $100,000 into $110,000, but have the potential of losing $15,000, leaving you with $85,000."

Your answer to these and others types of questions will help a financial professional determine what level of risk is right for you. They can then offer you investment strategies and management plans that reflect your financial age.

Take a moment to think about your income goals:

What is your lifestyle today? Would you like to maintain it into retirement? Are you meeting your needs? Are you happy with your lifestyle? What do you really *need* to live on when you retire? How are you going to structure your income flow during retirement?

Ultimately, crafting the retirement plan that is right for you is a numbers game: your risk tolerance is an important indicator of what kinds of investments you should consider, but if the returns from those investments don't meet your retirement goals, your income needs will likely not be met. For example, if the level of risk you are comfortable with manages your investments at a 4 percent return and you need to realize an 8 percent return, your income needs aren't going to be met when you need to rely on your investments for retirement income. The truth of the matter is that some people will have the luxury of maintaining or improving their lifestyle, while others may have to make decisions about what they need versus what they want during their retirement. If the numbers say that you need to be more aggressive with your investing, or that you need to modify your lifestyle, it becomes a choice you need to make.

Organizing your assets, understanding the color of your money, and creating an income and accumulation plan for retirement can quickly become an overwhelming task. The fact of the matter is that financial professionals build their careers around understanding the different variables affecting retirement financing. A professional may encourage you to be more aggressive with your investment strategy by taking on more risk in order to give you the potential of earning a greater return. If taking more risk isn't an option that you are comfortable with, then the discussion will turn to how you can earn more money or spend less in order to align your needs with your resources more closely.

Enlisting the help of a Registered Investment Advisor means working with a professional who is legally obligated to help you make financial decisions that are in your best interest and fall within your comfort zone. Taking steps toward creating a retirement plan is nothing to take lightly. By leveraging tax strategies, properly organizing your assets, and accumulating helpful financial products that help you meet your income and accumulation needs, you are more likely to meet your goals. You might have a million dollars socked away in a savings account, but your neighbor, who has $300,000 in a diverse investment portfolio that is tailored to their needs, may end up enjoying a better retirement lifestyle. Why? They had more than a good work ethic and a penchant for saving. They had a planful approach to retirement asset allocation.

CHAPTER 2 RECAP //

- There are two types of money: Green and Red. Green Money represents assets that are "safer" and more reliable. Red Money represents assets that are exposed to risk.
- There are two types of Green Money: *Need Now Money* and *Need Later Money*. It is important to structure your investments so that your assets will be capable of providing you with immediate income and the income you will need farther down the road.
- Working with a Registered Investment Advisor will help you compose a clear and concise inventory of your assets, and learn how much they are worth, what rules apply to them, and how they are structured for risk.
- A Registered Investment Advisor can help you structure your investments so as to reflect your risk tolerance.
- Working with an Investment Advisor means working with a professional who is legally obligated to help you make financial decisions that are in your best interest and fall within your comfort zone.
- The foundation of a retirement strategy depends on knowing how much money you need and when you need it.

3

Understanding Social Security

One kind of Green Money that most Americans can rely on for income when they retire is Social Security. If you're like most Americans, Social Security is or will be an important part of your retirement income and one that you should know how to properly manage. As a first step in creating your income plan, a financial professional will take a look at your Social Security benefit options. Social Security is the foundation of income planning for anyone who is about to retire and is a reliable source of Green Money in your overall income plan.

> » *Julia got her first job when she was 14 years old and she has been working steadily ever since. She enjoyed her career but she had been looking forward to retirement for many years*

31

so she could finally enjoy herself and her family more. This meant that she decided to file for her Social Security benefits as soon as they became available to her. Considering all the time she got to spend with her grandchildren and the rest of her family, it was a decision she thought she'd never regret.

However, several years later, Julia and her husband began to realize money was getting a little tight and they had to make some fairly significant changes to their lifestyle. As they went through the process of reorganizing their finances and creating a new household budget, Julia came across several old Social Security statements. She remembered how excited and ready she had been to put working full-time behind her so she could begin the next chapter of her life that she hadn't paid much attention to the details of her Social Security benefit.

As she looked over the old statements, she wondered if she would have been better off waiting to file for her benefits. It was an option she had never looked into because there had been so many other variables to consider and decisions to make during the retirement process. She decided to look into it and see if she would be eligible to change her monthly benefit to a higher amount.

Most unfortunately for Julia, she probably could have received a higher monthly benefit if she had waited to file for her Social Security benefits but it is far too late for her to change that now: once you file for Social Security and begin collecting your monthly benefit, you are permanently locked into that amount. The only exception to this rule is if you have received less than 12 months of payment, you could repay all your benefit checks and then defer filing so you would be able to reapply later, when your benefits might be higher. However, it is very difficult to take advantage of this loophole because most people can't afford to repay in one lump sum all the benefit checks they have received.

In other words, there is more to filing for your Social Security benefit than just filling out the correct paperwork. Your Social Security benefit is one of the best streams of income for you to tap into during your retirement. In fact, it will probably form the foundation of your plan because for every dollar you get from your Social Security benefit, that is one less dollar that has to be pulled from your nest egg to be used as Need Now income. Instead, that money can be put to work in other places. However, just like any other financial vehicle, if you want to get the most mileage out of your Social Security benefit, you need to understand how it works and what you need it to do. Unfortunately, this is a step many people fail to take. As the facts below infer, most people use Social Security but few people use it well:

- 90 percent of Americans age 65 and older receive Social Security benefits.*
- Social Security provides 39 percent of income for retired Americans.*
- Claiming Social Security benefits at the wrong time can reduce your monthly benefit by up to 57 percent.**
- 43 percent of men and 48 percent of women claim Social Security benefits at age 62.**
- 74 percent of retirees receive reduced Social Security benefits.**
- In 2013, the average monthly Social Security benefit was $1,261. *The maximum benefit for 2013 was $2,533. The $1,272 monthly benefit reduction between the average and the maximum is applied for life.***

---

*http://www.ssa.gov/pressoffice/basicfact.htm

**When to Claim Social Security Benefits, David Blanchett, CFA, CFP® January, 2013

***http://www.socialsecurity.gov/pressoffice/factsheets/colafacts2013.com

There are many aspects of Social Security that are well known and others that aren't. When it comes time for you to cash in on your Social Security benefit, you will have many options and choices. Social Security is a massive government program that manages retirement benefits for millions of people. Experts spend their entire careers understanding and analyzing it. Luckily, you don't have to understand all of the intricacies of Social Security to maximize its advantages. You simply need to know the best way to manage your Social Security benefit. You need to know exactly what to do to get the most from your Social Security benefit and when to do it. Taking the time to create a roadmap for your Social Security strategy will help ensure that you are able to exact your maximum benefit and efficiently coordinate it with the rest of your retirement plan.

There are many aspects of Social Security that you have no control over. You don't control how much you put into it, and you don't control what it's invested in or how the government manages it. However, you do control when and how you file for benefits. The real question about Social Security that you need to answer is, "When should I start taking Social Security?" While this is the all-important question, there are a couple of key pieces of information you need to track down first.

Before we get into a few calculations and strategies that can make all the difference, let's start by covering the basic information about Social Security which should give you an idea of where you stand. Just as the foundation of a house creates the stable platform for the rest of the framework to rest upon, your Social Security benefit is an important part of your overall retirement plan. The purpose of the information that follows is not to give an exhaustive explanation of how Social Security works, but to give you some tools and questions to start understanding how Social Security affects your retirement and how you can prepare for it.

Eligibility. Understanding how and when you are eligible for Social Security benefits will help clarify what to expect when the time comes to claim them.

To receive retirement benefits from Social Security, you must earn eligibility. In almost all cases, Americans born after 1929 must earn 40 quarters of credit to be eligible to draw their Social Security retirement benefit. In 2013, a Social Security credit represents $1,160 earned in a calendar quarter. The number changes as it is indexed each year, but not drastically. In 2012, a credit represented $1,130. Four quarters of credit is the maximum number that can be earned each year. In 2013, an American would have had to earn at least $4,640 to accumulate four credits. In order to qualify for retirement benefits, you must have earned a minimum number of credits. Additionally, if you are at least 62 years old and have been married to a recipient of Social Security benefits for at least 12 months, you can choose to receive Spousal Benefits. Although 40 is the minimum number of credits required to begin drawing benefits, it is important to know that once you claim your Social Security benefit, there is no going back. Although there may be cost of living adjustments made, you are locked into that base benefit amount forever.

Primary Insurance Amount. You can think of your Primary Insurance Amount (PIA) like a ripening fruit. It represents the amount of your Social Security benefit at your Full Retirement Age (FRA). Your benefit becomes fully ripe at your FRA, and will neither reduce nor increase due to early or delayed retirement options. If you opt to take benefits before your FRA, however, your monthly benefit will be less than your PIA. You will essentially be picking an unripened fruit. On the one hand, waiting until after your FRA to access your benefits will increase your benefit beyond your PIA. On the other hand, you don't want the fruit to overripen, because every month you wait is one less check you get from the government.

Full Retirement Age. Your FRA is an important figure for anyone who is planning to rely on Social Security benefits in their retirement. Depending on when you were born, there is a specific age at which you will attain FRA. Your FRA is dictated by your year of birth and is the age at which you can begin your full monthly benefit. Your FRA is important because it is half of the equation used to calculate your Social Security benefit. The other half of the equation is based on when you start taking benefits.

When Social Security was initially set up, the FRA was age 65, and it still is for people born before 1938. But as time has passed, the age for receiving full retirement benefits has increased. If you were born between 1938 and 1960, your full retirement age is somewhere on a sliding scale between 65 and 67. Anyone born in 1960 or later will now have to wait until age 67 for full benefits. Increasing the FRA has helped the government reduce the cost of the Social Security program, which pays out more than a half trillion dollars to beneficiaries every year!*

While you can begin collecting benefits as early as age 62, the amount you receive as a monthly benefit will be less than it would be if you wait until you reached your FRA or surpass your FRA. It is important to note that if you file for Social Security benefit before your FRA, *the reduction to your monthly benefit will remain in place for the rest of your life.* You can also delay receiving benefits up to age 70, in which case your benefits will be higher than your PIA for the rest of your life.

- At FRA, 100 percent of PIA is available as a monthly benefit.

---

*http://www.ssa.gov/pressoffice/basicfact.htm

- At age 62, your Social Security retirement benefits are available. For each month you take benefits prior to your FRA, however, the monthly amount of your benefit is reduced. *This reduction stays in place for the rest of your life.*
- At age 70, your monthly benefit reaches its maximum. After you turn age 70, your monthly benefit will no longer increase.

Year of Birth	Full Retirement Age
1943-1954	66
1955	66 and 2 months
1956	66 and 4 months
1957	66 and 6 months
1958	66 and 8 months
1959	66 and 10 months
1960 or later	age 67*

GROWING YOUR BENEFIT

Your Social Security income "rolls up" the longer you wait to claim it. Your monthly benefit will continue to increase until you turn 70 years old. But because Social Security is the foundation of most people's retirement, many Americans feel that they don't have control over how or when they receive their benefits. As a matter of fact, only four percent of Americans wait until after their FRA to file for benefits! This trend persists, despite the fact that every dollar you increase your Social Security income by means less money you will have to spend from your nest egg to meet your retirement income needs! For many people, creating their Social Security strategy is the most important decision they can make to positively impact their retirement. *The difference between the*

---

http://www.ssa.gov/OACT/progdata/nra.html

best and worst Social Security decision can be tens of thousands of dollars over a lifetime of benefits—up to $170,000!

Deciding NOW or LATER: Following the above logic, it makes sense to wait as long as you can to begin receiving your Social Security benefit. However, the answer isn't always that simple. Not everyone has the option of waiting. Many people need to rely on Social Security on day one of their retirement. In fact, *nearly 50 percent of 62-year-old Americans file for Social Security benefits.* Why is this number so high? Some might need the income. Others might be in poor health and don't feel they will live long enough to make FRA worthwhile for themselves or their families. It is also possible, however, that the majority of folks taking an early benefit at age 62 are simply under-informed about Social Security. As you try to decide when you should file for Social Security, consider the points below before you make a decision:

File Immediately if You:
- Find your job is unbearable.
- Are willing to sacrifice retirement income.
- Are not healthy and need a reliable source of income.

Consider Delaying Your Benefit if You:
- Want to maximize your retirement income.
- Want to increase retirement benefits for your spouse.
- Are still working and like it.
- Are healthy and willing / able to wait to file.

So if you decide to wait, how long should you wait? Lots of people can put it off for a few years, but not everyone can wait until they are 70 years old. Your individual circumstances may be able to help you determine when you should begin taking Social Security. If you do the math, you will quickly see that between ages 62 and 70, there are 96 months in which you can file for your Social Security benefit. If you take into account those 96 months and the 96 months your spouse could also file for Social Security, the number of different strategies for structuring your benefit, you can easily end up with more than 20,000 different scenarios. It's safe to say this isn't the kind of math that most people can easily handle. Each month would result in a different benefit amount. The longer you wait, the higher your monthly benefit amount becomes. Each month you wait, however, is one less month that you receive a Social Security check.

The goal is to maximize your lifetime benefits. That may not always mean waiting until you can get the largest monthly payment. Taking the bigger picture into account, you want to find out how to get the most money out of Social Security over the number of years that you draw from it. Don't underestimate the power of optimizing your benefit: the difference between the BEST and WORST Social Security election can easily be between $30,000 to $50,000 in lifetime benefits. *The difference can be very substantial!*

If you know that every month you wait, your Social Security benefit goes up a little bit, and you also know that every month you wait, you receive one less benefit check, how do you determine where the sweet spot is that maximizes your benefits over your lifetime? Financial professionals have access to software that will calculate the best year and month for you to file for benefits based on your default life expectancy. You can further customize that information by estimating your life expectancy based on your health, habits and family history. If you can then create an income plan (we'll get into this later in the chapter) that helps you wait until the target date for you to file for Social Security, you can optimize your retirement income strategy to get the most out of your Social Security benefit. How can you calculate your life expectancy? Well, you don't know exactly how long you'll live, but you have a better idea than the government does. They rely on averages to make their calculations. ***You have much more personal information about your health, lifestyle and family history than they do.*** You can use that knowledge to game the system and beat all the other people who are making uninformed decisions by filing early for Social Security.

While you can and should educate yourself about how Social Security works, the reality is you don't need to know a lot of general information about Social Security in order to make choices about your retirement. What you do need to know is exactly ***what to do to maximize your benefit.*** Because knowing what you need to do has huge impacts on your retirement! For most Americans, Social Security is the foundation of income planning for retirement. Social Security benefits represent nearly 40 percent of the income of retirees.* For many people, it can represent the largest portion of their retirement income. Not treating your Social Security benefit as an asset and investment tool can lead to sub-optimization of your largest source of retirement income.

Let's take a look at an example that shows the impact of working with a financial professional to optimize Social Security benefits:

> » *Rafael and Zoe Lara met in college and have been together ever since. Rafael is 60 years old and Zoe is 56. They have both worked their whole lives and tucked money away whenever they were able. They are looking forward to retiring and being able to spend more time with their grandchildren and hopefully have the opportunity to take a couple trips they always put off. Recently, they met with Jada, their financial professional, to discuss retirement options. Jada told them one of the first things they need to do is find out what their Social Security benefits could be because that will form the base of*

---

*http://www.ssa.gov/pressoffice/basicfact.htm

their income plan. Jada and the clients logged onto the Social Security website together to look up their PIAs and they found out Rafael's PIA is $1,900, while Zoe's PIA is $900.

If the Laras decide to file for their Social Security benefits as soon as they are able to, in other words, when they each turn 62 years old, Jada estimates they will receive approximately $492,000 in lifetime benefits. Initially, this sounds like plenty of money, but the Laras quickly realize that's only because they're thinking of it as a lump sum. As soon as they break it down a bit, the true limitations of that amount become apparent: if that amount is divided over 20 years, that would result in an annual income that is a little less than $25,000 per year. This is significantly lower than the annual income to which the Laras are accustomed. In order to make up the difference, the Laras would have to depend on other retirement income options to supplement their Social Security benefit. In other words, if they wanted to be able to maintain their current lifestyle, they would need to have a much bigger nest egg in order to generate the annual income they need.

However, if they chose not to file for their Social Security benefits right away and instead waited until they reached their FRA, Jada estimates their lifetime benefits would increase to $523,000. In doing so, they would achieve their Primary Insurance Amount and their annual income would increase to $33,000.

Even better than this is that, as a financial professional, Jada doesn't have to solely rely on the Social Security website for the Lara's benefit estimations. After spending a little more time talking with them to gain a better understanding of the Laras' situation, Jada then used software to calculate the most beneficial time for the Laras to begin drawing benefits. Through the use of this software, not only do Jada and the Lara's discover precisely the best time for them to file but, if *they were to file at this time, their potential lifetime benefits would drastically increase: the Laras could earn $660,000 in benefits!*

*If they follow Jada's advice, the Laras will be able to increase their potential lifetime benefits by as much as **$148,000**. This will have a profound impact on the type of retirement plan the Laras will develop and the future they will have.*

*By using strategies that their financial professional recommended, they increased their potential lifetime benefits by as much as **$148,000**. There's no telling how much you could miss out on from your Social Security if you don't take time to create a strategy that calculates your maximum benefit. For the Laras, the value of maximizing their benefits was the difference between night and day. While this may seem like a special case, it isn't uncommon to find benefit increases of this magnitude. You'll never know unless you take a look at your own options.*

As this example illustrates, there's no telling how much you could miss out on from your Social Security if you don't take time to create a strategy that calculates your maximum benefit. For the Laras, the value of maximizing their benefits was the difference between night and day. While this may seem like a special case, it isn't uncommon to find benefit increases of this magnitude if you know where to look. Of course, if you never take a moment to examine your Social Security benefit options, you'll never know if you're making the best decision or just the most apparent one.

So, to whom should you turn for advice when making this complex decision? Before you pick up the phone and call Uncle Sam, you should know that the Social Security Administration (SSA) representatives are actually prohibited from giving you election advice! Plus, SSA representatives in general are trained to focus on monthly benefit amounts, not the lifetime income for a family.

MAXIMIZING YOUR LIFETIME BENEFIT

As discussed earlier, calculating how to maximize **lifetime benefits** is more important than waiting until age 70 for your maximum **monthly benefit amount.** It's about getting the most income during your lifetime. Professional benefit maximization software can target the year and month that it is most beneficial for you to file based on your life expectancy.

The three most common ages that people associate with retirement benefits are 62 (Earliest Eligible Age), 66 (Full Retirement Age), and 70 (age at which monthly maximum benefit is reached). In almost all circumstances, however, none of those three most common ages will give you the maximum lifetime benefit.

Remember, every month you wait to file, the amount of your benefit check goes up, but you also get one less check. You don't know how exactly how long you're going to live, but you have a better idea of your life expectancy than the actuaries at the Social Security Administration who can only work with averages. They can't make calculations based on your specific situation. A professional can run the numbers for you and get the target date that maximizes your potential lifetime benefits. You can't get this information from the SSA, but you *can* get it from a financial professional.

Your Social Security options don't stop here, however. There are a plethora of other choices you can make to manipulate your benefit payments.

Just a Few Types of Social Security Benefits:
- *Retired Worker Benefit.* This is the benefit with which most people are familiar. The Retired Worker Benefit is what most people are talking about when they refer to Social

Security. It is your benefit based on your earnings and the amount that you have paid into the system over the span of your career.

- *Spousal Benefit.* The Spousal Benefit is available to the spouse of someone who is eligible for Retired Worker Benefits. What if there was a way for your spouse to receive his or her benefit for four years and not lose the chance to get his or her maximum benefit when he or she turns age 70? Many people do not know about this strategy and might be missing out on benefits they have earned.
- *Survivorship Benefit.* When one spouse passes away, the survivor is able to receive the larger of the two benefit amounts.
- *File and Suspend.* This concept allows for a lower-earning spouse to receive up to 50 percent of the other's PIA amount if both spouses file for benefits at the right time.
- *Restricted Application.* A higher-earning spouse may be able to start collecting a spousal benefit on the lower-earning spouse's benefit while allowing his or her benefit to continue to grow.

THE DIVORCE FACTOR

How does a divorced spouse qualify for benefits? If you have gone through a divorce, it might affect the retirement benefit to which you are entitled.

A person can receive benefits as a divorced spouse on a former spouse's Social Security record if he or she:

- Was married to the former spouse for at least 10 years;
- Is at least age 62 years old;
- Is unmarried; and

- Is not entitled to a higher Social Security benefit on his or her own record.*

With all of the different options, strategies and benefits to choose from, you can see why filing for Social Security is more complicated than just mailing in the paperwork. Gathering the data and making yourself aware of all your different options isn't enough to know exactly what to do, however. On the one hand, you can knock yourself out trying to figure out which options are best for you and wondering if you made the best decision. On the other hand, you can work with a financial professional who uses customized software that takes all the variables of your specific situation into account and calculates your best option. You have tens of thousands of different options for filing for your Social Security benefit. If your spouse is a different age than you are, it nearly doubles the amount of options you have. This is far more complicated arithmetic than most people can do on their own. If you want a truly accurate understanding of when and how to file, you need someone who will ask you the right questions about your situation, someone who has access to specialized software that can crunch the numbers. The reality is that you need to work with a professional that can provide you with the sophisticated analysis of your situation that will help you make a truly informed decision.

Important Questions about Your Social Security Benefit:
- How can I maximize my lifetime benefit? By knowing when and how to file for Social Security. This usually means waiting until you have at least reached your Full Retirement Age. A professional has the experience and the

---

*http://www.ssa.gov/retire2/yourdivspouse.htm

tools to help determine when and how you can maximize your lifetime benefits.

- Who will provide reliable advice for making these decisions? Only a professional has the tools and experience to provide you reliable advice.
- Will the Social Security Administration provide me with the advice? The Social Security Administration cannot provide you with advice or strategies for claiming your benefit. They can give you information about your monthly benefit, but that's it. They also don't have the tools to tell you what your specific best option is. They can accurately answer how the system works, but they can't advise you on what decision to make as to how and when to file for benefits.

The Maximization Report that your financial professional will generate represents an invaluable resource for understanding how and when to file for your Social Security benefit. When you get your customized Social Security Maximization Report, you will not only know all the options available to you—but you will understand the financial implications of each choice. In addition to the analysis, you will also get a report that shows *exactly* at what age—including which month and year—you should trigger benefits and how you should apply. It also includes a variety of other time-specific recommendations, such as when to apply for Medicare or take Required Minimum Distributions from your qualified plans. A report means there is no need to wonder, or to try to figure out when to take action—the Social Security Maximization Report lays it all out for you in plain English.

CHAPTER 3 RECAP //

- Once you file for your Social Security benefit, you will be permanently locked into that amount so be sure that you only file when you're confident you're doing so at the time that is most beneficial for you and your family.
- To make sure you are getting the most out of your Social Security benefit, you need to be filing at both the right time and in the right way. There are thousands of different permutations when it comes to filing for Social Security. Financial professionals have access to software that can precisely calculate the most optimum way for you to make this decision.
- Every dollar you get from your Social Security benefit is one less dollar that has to come from your nest egg, which means you can put that money to work for you in different and more beneficial ways.
- Be aware that your Social Security benefit is subject to taxes.

4

Going the Distance: Filling the Income Gap

Recall that the moment that you stop working and start living off the money that you've set aside for retirement can be referred to as the "Retirement Cliff." You've worked and earned money your whole life, but the day that you retire, that income comes to an end. That's the day that you have to have other assets that fill the gap. Social Security will fill in some, but you need to come up with something else. After you have calculated your Social Security benefit and have selected the year and month that will maximize your lifetime benefits, it's time to look at your other retirement assets, incomes and options that will reduce or eliminate the dropoff of the Retirement Cliff. You may have a pension, an IRA or Roth IRA, dividends from stock holdings, money from the sale of real estate, rental property, or other sources of income. What other sources of reliable income do you have?

If your monthly Social Security check and your other supplemental income leaves a shortfall in your *desired* income, how are you going to fix it? This shortfall is called the **Income Gap** and it needs to be filled in order to maintain your lifestyle into retirement. If you have a known income gap that you need to fill, you want to know how to fill that income gap with the fewest dollars possible. You basically want to buy that income gap for the least amount of money possible. You don't want it to cost you too much, because you want to get the most out of your other assets, including planning for your future and planning for your legacy. You do that by maximizing your Social Security benefit, leveraging your additional income and looking at other investment tools that can help generate income for you. Your specific needs, of course, should be analyzed by a professional.

Today, you probably have savings in a variety of assets that you have acquired over the years. But you may not have taken time to examine them and assess how they will support your retirement. However, it is crucial that you engage with this process of examination because it's not a question of *if* the market will go up or down, but *when* it will and if it goes down at the wrong time for your five or 10-year retirement horizon, you could be in serious danger of losing some of your retirement income.

By creating an income plan before you retire you can avoid this problem by gaining a clear understanding of your financial needs and developing a sustainable strategy that will satisfy them in the most efficient way possible. Doing so will give more security to your Need Later Money and will potentially allow you to build your legacy down the road. Ultimately, creating an income plan will help to ensure that your lifestyle can last as long as you do.

» Aiko will be celebrating her 60th birthday this year and she wants to be retired by the time she celebrates her 70th. To that end, she recently sat down and crunched some numbers and realized that after her Social Security benefit, she will still need nearly $375,000 to generate a modest annual income of $40,000. Aiko is dumbfounded: she would have never imagined that she'd need that much money to support what she considers to be a fairly conservative lifestyle. She has few ideas about how she will be able to make up for this shortfall. When her daughter visits the following month, Aiko mentions the surprising news and expresses her desire to be able to put more money into Social Security so she would be able to get more out of it later and secure a guaranteed income. If that were a possibility, it would be the perfect Green Money asset for her retirement! Aiko's daughter explains that a Green Money asset like that does exist and it's called an annuity.

ANNUITIES: A GOOD FIT FOR YOU?

An annuity is a financial tool that is similar to Social Security in that it is capable of providing you with a reliable source of income. Unlike Social Security, however, annuities also have the potential to increase the value of your principal investment. If you have assets that you would like to structure for retirement income, **an annuity may be the right choice for you.**

Consider the following questions:

- How concerned are you about finding a secure financial vehicle to protect your savings?
- How concerned are you that there may be a better way to structure your savings?

If alleviating these concerns is a top priority for you, an income annuity investment tool would likely be an invaluable component for you to include within your retirement plan. Income annuities have many qualities similar to Social Security that give them the same look and feel as that reliable benefit check you get every month. Most importantly, an income annuity can be an efficient and profitable way to solve your income gap.

HOW ANNUITIES FIT INTO AN OVERALL INCOME PLAN

Annuities are flexible financial vehicles that you can use to tailor your retirement plan so it will be able to meet your current and future income needs. Although the term "annuity" may be new to you, the concept is old and one with which you are very much familiar. In its most elementary form, an "annuity" is simply a way to invest your money that allows you to structure it for income. This can be accomplished utilizing a plethora of different methods and means, which makes the field of annuities an incredibly broad one. For example, both your Social Security benefit and winnings from a State Lottery are both technically annuities because they organize your investment into a series of income distributions. For our purposes, however, we use the term "annuity" to refer specifically to the financial product sold by insurance companies. When you put your money into an annuity, you are essentially buying a contract between you and the insurance company and it is this contract that provides the investment tool. While there are many different types of annuities, each promoting their own diverse array of benefits and features, one of the most common advantages of an annuity is one of its most appealing, as well: it provides a place to invest your money that allows it to keep pace with inflation but not at the expense of its security. Thus, by working with a financial professional you will be able to select the annuity that is best suited to meeting your needs. Before you invest in money in an annuity always be sure that you fully comprehend all of its associated features, benefits, and costs.

Let's say you have saved $100,000 and need it to generate income to meet your needs above and beyond your Social Security and pension checks. You give the $100,000 to an insurance company, who in turn invests it to generate growth. They usually select investments that have modest returns over long-term horizons. In other words, they generally put it somewhere stable and predictable. Most commonly, they will invest it in a combination of bonds and treasuries that are safer and dependable ways to grow money. They use the money from the insurance products they sell to invest, use a portion of the returns to generate profits for themselves, and return a portion to clients in the form of payouts, claims, and structured income options.

One of the most attractive qualities of these types of annuities is something called annual reset. Annual reset is sometimes also referred to as a "ratcheting." Instead of taking on the risk that comes with putting money in a fluctuating market, you can offset that risk onto the insurance company. It works like this: If the market goes down, you don't suffer a loss. Instead, the insurance company absorbs it. But if the market goes up, you share with the insurance company some of the profit made on the gain. The amount of gain you get is called your annuity participation rate. Typically the insurer will cap the amount of gain you can realize at somewhere between 3 and 7 percent. If the market goes up 10 percent, you would realize a portion of that gain (whatever percentage you are capped at). This means you to never lose money on your investment, while always gaining a portion of the upswings. The measurement period of your annuity can be calculated monthly, weekly and even daily, but most annuities are measured annually. The level of the index when you buy and the index level one year later will determine the amount of loss or gain. You and the insurance company are betting that the market will generally go up over time.

TAKING YOUR ANNUITY FOR A RIDE

Keep in mind that annuities are, at their core, insurance products, which means that just like you can purchase additional coverage for your auto or homeowner's insurance policy to better make it suit your needs, you can do the same thing with an annuity. The additional benefit that you purchase separately from the base policy is what the term "rider" refers to. An income rider is probably the most common way to customize an annuity. Let's continue on with our example to see how it can work:

When you use that $100,000 to buy a contract with an insurance company in the form of an annuity, you are pegging your money on an index. It could be the S&P 500, the Dow Jones Industrial Average or any number of indexes. To generate income from the annuity, you select something called an income rider. An income rider is a subset of an indexed annuity. Essentially, it is the amount of money from which the insurance company will pay you an income while you have your money in their annuity. Your income rider is a larger number than what your investment is actually worth, and if you select the income rider, it will increase in value over time, providing you with more income. As the insurance company holds your money and invests it, they generate a return on it that they use to pay you a regular monthly income based on a higher number. The insurance company has to outperform the amount that they pay you in order to make a profit.

Remember, insurance companies make long-term investments that provide them with predictable flows of money. They like to stabilize the amount of money that goes in and out of their doors instead of paying and receiving large unpredictable chunks at once. When you opt for an income rider, an insurance company can reliably predict how much money they will pay out to you over a set period of time. It's predictable, and they like that. They can base their business on those predictable numbers.

In order to encourage investors to leave their money in their annuity contracts, insurance companies create surrender periods that protect their investments. If you remove your money from the annuity contract during the surrender period, you will pay a penalty and will not be able to receive your entire investment amount back. A typical surrender period is 10 years. If after three years you decide that you want your $100,000 back, the insurance company has that money tied up in bonds and other investments with the understanding that they will have it for another seven years. Because they will take a hit on removing the money from their investments prematurely, you will have to pay a surrender charge that makes up for their loss. During the surrender period, an annuity is not a demand deposit account like a savings or checking account. The higher returns that you are guaranteed from an annuity are dependent on the timeframe you selected.

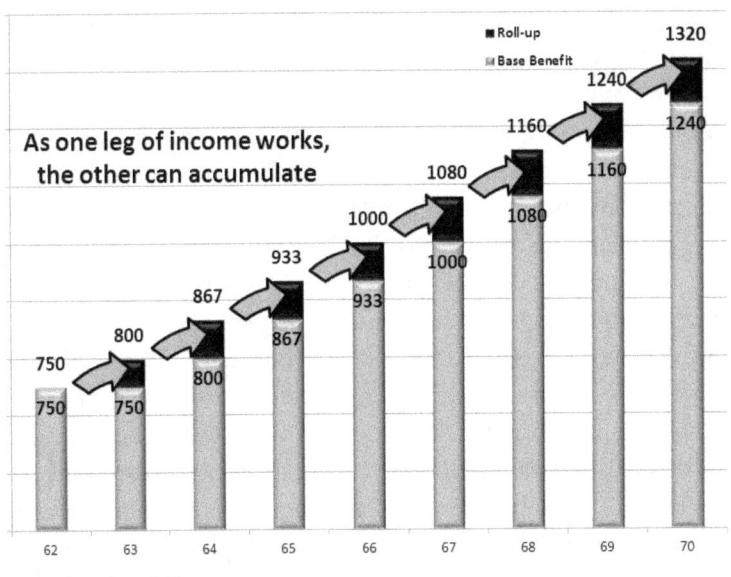

This is a hypothetical illustration

The longer an insurance company can hold your money, the easier it is for them to guarantee a predictable return on it.

If you leave your money in the annuity contract, you get a reliable monthly income no matter what happens in the market. Once the surrender period has expired, you can remove your money whenever you want. Your money becomes liquid again because the insurance company has used it in an investment that fit the timeline of your surrender period. For many people, this is an attractive trade off that can provide a creative solution for filling their income gap.

When is an annuity with an income rider right for you? A good financial professional can help you make that determination by taking the time to listen closely to your situation and understanding what your needs are as you enter retirement. Moreover, a financial professional can help you make a selection from the many other riders you can use to modify an annuity so it will be uniquely customized to fit your particular situation and needs. As you know, it's never too early to begin planning ahead so as you consider what annuity might be right for you, don't limit yourself to thinking of it as only an additional income source: annuities can also be useful for your legacy and the organization of your estate. For instance, if you select a Death Benefit Rider your annuity will be able to do double-duty as both a retirement tool and a legacy-planning tool because it allows you to select a beneficiary for your annuity. Additionally, some Death Benefit Riders will even guarantee the amount of money that the annuity will payout to the beneficiary so you can be sure your heirs will get the most value out of your investment. Moreover, a critical care rider can be used to help offset costs associated with healthcare. Not only do these riders help to ensure that you receive the best healthcare available to you, but they also help to preserve your legacy by making sure that your assets won't be depleted by healthcare costs as you near the end of your life. Additionally, they can be a particularly useful option for individuals who either can't afford a long-term healthcare option or who were not able to qualify because of their health.

Every salesperson has a bag full of brochures and PowerPoint presentations, but they need to know exactly what the financial concerns of their individual clients are in order to help them make the most informed and beneficial decision. Some people need income today, others need it in five or 10 years. Others may have their income needs met but are planning to move closer to their children and will need to buy a house in 10 years. Or, if you want income in 15 years, you might want to choose a different investment product for 10 years, and then switch to an annuity with an income rider during the last five years of your timeline. Everyone's situation is different and everyone's needs are different. An annuity is an excellent tool to use for people interested in designing a distinctively personalized retirement plan because they are flexible and capable of producing a guaranteed income stream, which will help you better secure you and your family's future. Talking to a financial professional is the best way to find out which annuity need and if you need to use a rider to provide you with additional coverage.

AN ANNUITY BUILT FOR YOU

There are several different kinds of annuities to choose from depending on the requirements of your financial circumstance and your risk tolerance:

Fixed Annuities pay guaranteed rates of interest, which makes them function almost like a Certificate of Deposit (CD) except that they pay out at a higher rate. For example, a fixed five-year annuity is paying at a tax deferred rate of about 3.5 percent. Essentially, fixed annuities are a good way to "beat the bank" without risking your principal investment.

Fixed Index Annuities increase at rates determined by the market: if the market does well, a fixed index annuity may result in higher yields than either a CD or a fixed annuity. While fixed index annuities rates of growth are linked to the market, this does not mean fixed index annuities *vary* with the market because if the market does poorly you do not suffer a loss to your principal. By attaching an income rider, this can provide lifelong guaranteed income.

Variable Annuities, however, do vary with the market, which means they can lose money according to market fluctuations. These annuities do not take advantage of annual reset when the market goes down. The income rider will stay the same, but the value of your actual contract may fall. If you surrender the annuity, the insurance company will pay you the market value of the asset, regardless of whether it matches, exceeds or falls short of the value at which you bought the contract. If its value has dropped significantly, you may be better off taking the income rider without surrendering your contract. In most cases, selecting a variable annuity is not recommended because a fixed index annuity can often provide similar benefits but with less risk. For example, the rate of return for most variable annuities is currently hovering between about 3-5 percent, which is similar to what you can expect from a fixed index annuity. Consequently, it often makes more sense to go with the safer option and choose a fixed index annuity. What's more is that a variable annuity is tied to one specific fund, which means its rate of return is reliant upon the performance of a few specific stocks, whereas a fixed index annuity is tied to the market as a whole so its rate of return is more diversified. It's important to be aware of the risks associated with variable annuities and know that they may not be advisable for investors who are drawn to annuities because of their income generating capabilities.

Single Premium Immediate Annuities (SPIA) are structured so that you pay a lump sum of money (a single premium) to an insurance company, and they immediately begin giving you a guaranteed income over an agreed upon time period, which could be as short as five years or as long as the remainder of your lifetime. SPIAs provide investors with a stream of reliable income when they can't afford to take the risk of losing money in a fluctuating market. While there is general faith that the market always trends up, at least in the long-term, if you are focusing on income over a shorter period of time, you may not be able to take a big hit in the market. Beyond normal market volatility, interest rates also come with an inherent level of uncertainty, making it hard to create a dependable income on your own. SPIAs reduce risk for you by giving you regular monthly, quarterly or yearly payments that can begin the moment you buy the contract.

ANNUITIES AT WORK

Ultimately, annuities are investment tools that look and feel a bit like Social Security: every year you allow the money to grow with the market, and it will "roll up" by a specific amount, paying out a specific percent to you as income each year. For most people, taking a large financial risk once they've retired is an incredibly stressful notion. Annuities are insurance products that are versatile enough to meet the demands of most retirement plans and they do so in a safe and reliable manner. Just like with any investment strategy, however, be sure that your annuity is fulfilling a specific purpose and falls within your risk tolerance. Here are some general ways to manage risk within your annuity:

If you want to structure an annuity investment for moderate growth over a long period of time and create a guaranteed income source, you can select a fixed index annuity with an income rider. The value of your principal investment follows the market and will gain value up to a certain cap but will not suffer any loss if the market performs poorly. For example, a 40-year-old couple may select a fixed index annuity with an income rider that kicks in when they plan to retire. If it rises with the market or outperforms it, the value of their investment has grown. If the market loses ground over the duration of the contract or their annuity underperforms, they can still rely on the income rider and their principal investment.

If you are 68 years old and you have more immediate income needs that you need to come up with above and beyond your Social Security, you need a low risk, reliable source of income. If you choose an annuity option, you are looking for something that will pay out an income right away over a relatively short timeframe. You probably want to opt for a SPIA that pays you immediately and spans a five-year period, as well as an additional annuity that begins paying you in five years, and another longer term annuity that begins paying you in 10 years. Bear in mind that each annuity contract has its own costs and fees. Review these with your financial professional before you determine the best products and strategies for your situation.

The following example shows just how helpful an indexed annuity option can be for a retiree:

> » *Dorian and Selma are 62 years old and have decided to run the numbers to see what their retirement is going to look like. They know they currently need $6,000 per month to pay their bills and maintain their current lifestyle. They have also done their Social Security homework and have determined that, between the two of them, they will receive $4,200 per month in benefits. They also receive $350 per month in rent from a tenant who lives in a small carriage house in their backyard. Between their Social Security and the monthly rent income, they will be short $1,450 per month.*

They do have an additional asset, however. They have been contributing for years to an IRA that has reached a value of $350,000. They realize that they have to figure out how to turn the $350,000 in their IRA into $1,450 per month for the rest of their life. At first glance, it may seem like they will have plenty of money. With some quick calculations, they find they have 240 months, or nearly 20 years, of monthly income before they exhaust the account. When you consider income tax, the potential for higher taxes in the future, and market fluctuations (because many IRAs are invested in the market), the amount in the IRA seems to have a little less clout. Every dollar Dorian and Selma take out of the IRA is subject to income tax, and if they leave the remainder in the IRA, they run the risk of losing money in a volatile market. Once they retire and stop getting a paycheck every two weeks, they also stop contributing to their IRA. And when they aren't supplementing its growth with their own money, they are entirely dependent on market growth. That's a scary prospect. They could also withdraw the money from the IRA and put it in a savings account or CD, but removing all the money at once will put them in a tax bracket that will claim a huge portion of the value of the IRA. A seemingly straightforward asset has now become a complicated equation. Dorian and Selma didn't know what to do, so they met with their financial professional.

Their financial professional suggested that they use the money to purchase an indexed annuity with an income rider. They selected an annuity that was designed for their specific situation. They took the lump sum from their IRA, placed it in an indexed annuity taking advantage of annual reset so they never lost the value of their investment. In return, they were guaranteed the $1,450 of income per month that they needed to meet their retirement goals. The simplicity of the contract allowed them to do an analysis with their professional just once to understand the product. They basically put their money in an investment crockpot where they didn't have to look at it or manage it. They just needed to let it simmer. In fact, their professional was able to find an annuity for them that allowed them their $1,450 monthly payment with a lump sum of $249,455, leaving them more than $100,000 to reinvest somewhere else. Keep in mind that annuities are tax deferred, meaning you will pay tax on the income you receive from an annuity in the year you receive it.

» Cosima is 60 years old and is wondering how she can use her assets to provide her with a retirement income. She has a $5,000 per month income need. If she starts withdrawing her Social Security benefit in six years at age 66, it will provide her with $2,200 per month. She also has a pension that kicks in at age 70 that will give her another $1,320 per month.

That leaves an income gap of $2,800 from ages 66 to 69, and then an income gap of $1,480 at age 70 and beyond. If Cosima uses only Green Money to solve her income need, she will need to deposit $918,360 at 2 percent interest to meet her monthly goal for her lifetime. If she opts to use Red Money and withdraws the amount she needs each month from the market, let's say the S & P 500, she will run out of cash in 10 years if she invested between the years of 2000 and 2012. Suffering a market downturn like that during the period for which she is relying on it for retirement income will change her life, and not for the better.

Working with a financial professional to find a better way, Cosima found that she could take a hybrid approach to fill her income gap. Her professional recommended two different income vehicles: one that allowed her to deposit just $190,161 with a 2 percent return, and one that was a

$146,000 income annuity. These tools filled her income gap with $336,161, requiring her to spend $582,000 less money to accomplish her goal! Working with a professional to find the right tools for her retirement needs saved Cosima over half a million dollars.

As these examples illustrate, the many different types and features of annuities allow you to outfit them precisely according to your needs. There is no single way to use an annuity and working with a financial professional can help you select the type and method that will be best for you. Before we move forward, let's quickly review a basic outline of what we have covered thus far:

- Review your income needs and look specifically at the shortfall you may have during each year of your retirement based on your Social Security income, and income from any other assets you have.
- Ask yourself where you are in your distribution phase. Is retirement one year away? 10 years away? Last year?
- Determine how much money you need and how you need to structure your existing assets to provide for that need.
- If you have an asset from which you need to generate income, consider options offered by purchasing an income rider on an annuity.

CHAPTER 4 RECAP //

- Having an income plan will help you get a picture of what your retirement is really going to look like and by including your Social Security options within your income plan you will be able to see how much more money will be needed to support the lifestyle you desire.
- After Social Security and your additional income are accounted for, the amount that's left to meet your needs is called the *Income Gap*.
- It is important to find ways to leverage your retirement assets to satisfy your need for lifetime income.
- An annuity is a flexible and reliable investment tool that can help you fill your income gap. Not only can an annuity provide you with a guaranteed source of income but it also affords you the opportunity to grow your investment and it can accomplish both of these tasks without ever putting your principal investment at risk.
- Be sure you understand the features, benefits, costs and fees associated with any annuity product before you invest.

5

What is Yellow Money?

Understanding your Social Security benefit, filling the income gap and making an overall plan that meets your retirement income needs is no small task. Once you have worked with a financial professional to structure your income needs, it's time to take a look at the future. With your immediate income needs met, you have the opportunity to take your additional assets and leverage them for profit to supplement your income in the future, to prepare for anticipated health care costs or to contribute to your legacy. Stable income also means that you should have the staying power to stick with your investment portfolio through the ups and downs in the market.

Now that you've calculated the Rule of 100, determined how much risk you have and how much you want, and you've determined how much Green Money you need to meet your short-term and mid-term income needs, it's time to look at what you have left. The money you have left after you've calculated your Green Money needs has the potential of becoming Red Money: your stocks, mutual funds and other investment products that you want to continue accumulating value with the market. You now have the luxury of taking a closer second look at your Red Money to determine how you would like to manage it.

AN UNCERTAIN ALLY

A fickle market can raise the eyebrows of even the most veteran investor. This statement rings especially true, however, for an *individual* who is invested in the market. Taking a hit in the market hurts no matter how stable your income. Part of the pain comes from knowing that when you take a step back in the market, it requires an even larger step forward to return to where you were. As the market goes up and down, those larger gains you need to realize to get back to zero start to look even more daunting.

It can be challenging to watch the stock market's erratic changes every month, week or even every day. When you have your money riding on it, the ride can feel pretty bumpy. When you are managing your money by yourself, emotions inevitably enter into the mix. The Dow Jones Industrial Average and the S&P 500 represent more to you than market fluctuations. They represent a portion of your retirement. It's hard not to be emotional about it.

Everyone knows you should buy low and sell high. But this is what is more likely to happen:

The market takes a downturn, similar to the 2008 crash, and investors see as much as a 30 percent loss in their stock holdings. It's hard to watch, and it's harder to bear the pain of losing that much money. The math of rebounds means that they will need to rely on even larger gains just to get back to where things were before the downturn. They sell. But eventually, and inevitably, the market begins to rise again. Maybe slowly, maybe with some moderate growth, but by the time the average investor notices an upward trend and wants to buy in again, they have already missed a great deal of the gains.

YELLOW MONEY

As has been previously established, having some of your money be Red Money is, for all intents and purposes, essentially un-avoidable. Consequently, this begs the question: how much of your Red Money do you invest, and in what kinds of markets, investment products and stocks do you invest? There are a lot of different directions in which you can take your Red Money. One thing is for sure: significant accumulation depends on investing in the market. How you go about doing it is different for every-one. Gathering stocks, bonds and investment funds together in a portfolio without a cohesive strategy behind them could cause you to miss out on the benefits of a more thoughtful and planful approach. The end result is that you may never really understand what your money is doing, where and how it is really invested, and which investment principles are behind the investment products you hold. While you may have goals for each individual piece of your portfolio, it is likely that you don't have a comprehensive plan for your Red Money, which may mean that *you are taking on more risk than you would like, and are getting less return for it than is possible.*

Enter **Yellow Money.** Yellow Money is money that is man-aged by a professional *with a purpose.* After your income needs are met and you have assets that you would like to dedicate to accumulation, there are decisions you need to make about how to invest those assets. You can buy stocks, index funds, mutual funds, bonds — you name it — you can invest in it. However, the difference between Red Money and Yellow Money is that Yellow Money has a cohesive strategy behind it that is *implemented by a professional.* When you manage your Red Money with an invest-ment plan, it becomes Yellow Money: *money that is being managed* *with a specific purpose, a specific set of focused goals and a specific strategy in mind.* Yellow Money is still a type of Red Money. It comes with different levels of risk. But Yellow Money is under the watchful eye of professionals who have a stake in the success of your money in the market and who can recommend a range of strategies from those designed for preservation to those targeting rapid growth. You don't want to miss out on achieving the right level of risk, and more importantly, composing a careful plan for the return of your assets.

Yellow Money is generally Need Later Money that you want to grow for needs you'll have in at least 10 years. You can work with your financial planner to create investments that meet your needs within different timeframes. You may need to rely on some of your Yellow Money in 10, 15 or 20 years, whether for additional income, a large purchase you plan on making or a vacation. Whatever you want it for, you will need it down the road. A financial professional can help you rescale the risk of your assets as they grow, helping you lock in your profits and secure a source of income you can depend on later.

THE INDIVIDUAL INVESTOR AND MARKET VOLATILITY

To understand the importance of Yellow Money, let's take a closer look at the impact of volatility on the individual investor:

> » *Mariana's situation illustrates how market volatility can have major repercussions for an individual investor. Mariana has worked for Delta Pen Company for 30 years. During her time there, she acquires bonuses and pay raises that often include shares of stock in the company. She also dedicates part of her paycheck every month to a 401(k) that bought Delta stock. By the time she retires, Mariana has $250,000 worth of Acme stock.*

Although she had contributes to her 401(k) account every month, Mariana doesn't cultivate any other assets that could generate income for her during retirement. Mariana also retires early at age 62 because of her failing health. The commute to work every day was becoming difficult in her weakened condition and she wanted to enjoy the rest of her life in retirement instead of working at Acme.

Because she retires early, Mariana fails to maximize her Social Security benefit. While she lives a modest lifestyle, her income needs will still be $3,500 per month. Mariana's monthly Social Security check will only cover $1,900, leaving her with a $1,600 income gap. To supplement her Social Security check, Mariana sells $1,600 of her Delta stock each month to meet her income needs. A $250,000 401(k) is nothing to sneeze at, but reducing its value by $1,600 every month will barely last Mariana 10 years. And that's if the market stays neutral or grows modestly. If the market takes a downturn, the money that Mariana relied on to fill her income gap will rapidly diminish. Even if the market starts going up in a couple of years, it will take much larger gains for her to recover the value that she lost.

Unhappily for Mariana, she retired in 2007, just before the major market downturn that lasted for several years. She lost more than 20 percent of the value of her stock. Because Mariana needed to sell her stock to meet her basic income needs, the market price of the stock was secondary to her need for the money. When she needed money, she was forced to sell however many shares she needed to fill her income gap that month. And if she has a financial crisis, involving her need for medical care, for example, she will be forced to sell stock even if the market is low and her shares are nearly worthless.

Mariana realizes that she could have relied on an investment structured to deliver her a regular income while pro-

tecting the value of her investment. She could have kept her $250,000 from diminishing while enjoying her lifestyle into retirement regardless of the volatility of the market. Ideally, Mariana would have restructured her 401(k) to reflect the level of risk that she was able to take. In her case, she would have had most of her money in Green Money assets, allowing her to rely on the value of her assets when she needed them.

In 2013, DALBAR, the well-respected financial services market research firm, released their annual "Quantitative Analysis of Investment Behavior" report (QAIB). The report studied the impact of market volatility on individual investors: people like Mariana, or anyone who was managing (or mismanaging) their own investments in the stock market.

According to the study, volatility not only caused investors to make decisions based on their emotions, those decisions also harmed their investments and prevented them from realizing potential gains. So why do people meddle so much with their investments when the market is fluctuating? Part of the reason is that many people have financial obligations that they don't have control over. Significant expenses like house payments, the unexpected cost of replacing a broken-down car, and medical bills can put people in a position where they need money. If they need to sell investments to come up with that money, they don't have the luxury of selling when they *want* to. They must sell when they *need* to.

DALBAR's "Quantitative Analysis of Investor Behavior" has been used to measure the effects of investors' buying, selling and mutual fund switching decisions since 1994. The QAIB shows time and time again over nearly a 20 year period that the average investor earns less, and in many cases, significantly less than the performance of mutual funds suggests. QAIB's goal is to improve independent investor performance and to help financial professionals provide helpful advice and investment strategies that address the concerns and behaviors of the average investor.

An excerpt from the report claims that:*

"QAIB offers guidance on how and where investor behaviors can be improved. No matter what the state of the mutual fund industry, boom or bust: Investment results are more dependent on investor behavior than on fund performance. Mutual fund investors who hold on to their investments are more successful than those who time the market.

QAIB uses data from the Investment Company Institute (ICI), Standard & Poor's and Barclays Capital Index Products to compare mutual fund investor returns to an appropriate set of benchmarks.

There are actually three primary causes for the chronic shortfall for both equity and fixed income investors:

1. *Capital not available to invest. This accounts for 25 percent to 35 percent of the shortfall.*
2. *Capital needed for other purposes. This accounts for 35 percent to 45 percent of the shortfall.*
3. *Psychological factors. These account for 45 percent to 55 percent of the shortfall."*

The key findings of Dalbar's QAIB report provide compelling statistics about how individual investment strategies produced negative outcomes for the majority of investors:

- Psychological factors account for 45 percent to 55 percent of the chronic investment return shortfall for both equity and fixed income investors.
- Asset allocation is designed to handle the investment decision-making for the investor, which can materially reduce the shortfall due to psychological factors.

*2013 QAIB, Dalbar, March 2013

- Successful asset allocation investing requires investors to act on two critical imperatives:
- Balance capital preservation and appreciation so that they are aligned with the investor's objective.
- Select a qualified allocator.
- The best way for an investor to determine their risk tolerance is to utilize a risk tolerance assessment. However, these assessments must be accessible and usable.
- Evaluating allocator quality requires analysis of the allocator's underlying investments, decision making process and whether or not past efforts have produced successful outcomes.
- Choosing a top allocator makes a significant difference in the investment results one will achieve.
- Mutual fund retention rates suggest that the average investor has not remained invested for long enough periods to derive the potential benefits of the investment markets.
- Retention rates for asset allocation funds exceed those of equity and fixed income funds by over a year.
- Investors' ability to correctly time the market is highly dependent on the direction of the market. Investors generally guess right more often in up markets. However, in 2012 investors guessed right only 42 percent of the time during a bull market.
- Analysis of investor fund flows compared to market performance further supports the argument that investors are unsuccessful at timing the market. Market upswings rarely coincide with mutual fund inflows while market downturns do not coincide with mutual fund outflows.
- Average equity mutual fund investors gained 15.56 percent compared to a gain of 15.98 percent that just holding the S&P 500 produced.

- The shortfall in the long-term annualized return of the average mutual fund equity investor and the S&P 500 continued to decrease in 2012.
- The fixed-income investor experienced a return of 4.68 percent compared to an advance of 4.21 percent on the Barclays Aggregate Bond Index.
- The average fixed income investor has failed to keep up with inflation in nine out of the last 14 years.*

It doesn't take a financial services market research report to tell you that market volatility is out of your control. The report does prove, however, that before you experience market volatility, you should have an investment plan, and when the market is fluctuating, you should stand by your investment plan. You should also review and discuss your investment plan with your financial professional on a regular basis, ensuring he/she is aware of any changes in your goals, financial circumstances, your health or your risk tolerance. When the economy is under stress and the markets are volatile, investors can feel vulnerable. That vulnerability causes people to tinker with their portfolios in an attempt to outsmart the market. Financial professionals, however, don't try to time the market for their clients. They try to tap into the gains that can be realized by committing to long-term investment strategies.

Clearly, the market is not an easy realm for an individual investor to inhabit, which helps to underscore the importance of Yellow Money. It can be helpful to think of Red Money and Yellow Money with this analogy:

If you needed to travel through an unfamiliar city in a foreign country, you could rent a car or perhaps hire a driver. Were you to drive yourself, you would try to gain guidance from perplexing road signs and need to adhere to traffic rules—with no experience

2013 QAIB, Dalbar, March 2013

or assistance to lean on. It would take longer to get to where you want to go, and the chance of a traffic accident would be higher. If you hired a driver, they would manage your journey. A driver would know the route, how to avoid traffic, and follow the rules of the road.

Red Money is like driving yourself. With Yellow Money, you are still traveling by car, but now you have a professional working on your behalf.

CHAPTER 5 RECAP //

- When it comes to playing the market, the deck is stacked against the individual investor because it's hard to separate your emotions from your investment decisions and to stay invested in the market long enough to be able to reap the benefits.
- In order to maintain a portfolio that is robust enough to sustain your financial needs, however, some of your money must be in the market and therefore at risk.
- By making sure your Red Money is Yellow Money, which means that it is professionally and purposefully managed, you can mitigate your exposure to risk.
- Having Yellow Money means your assets will be in financial vehicles that are both riskier and potentially more profitable, but they will be carefully managed according to the specific investment strategy you and your financial professional devise.

6

Putting Yellow Money to Work

Now that you know what Yellow Money is and understand the vital role it will play in your portfolio, let's consider how you can change the color of your money from red to yellow. As you read earlier in the key findings of the DALBAR report, the deck is stacked against the individual investor. Remember that the average investor on a fixed income failed to keep pace with inflation in nine of the last 14 years, meaning the inherent risk in managing your Red Money·is very real and could have a lasting impact on your assets.

PUTTING YOUR PORTFOLIO UNDER THE MICROSCOPE

Think about your investment portfolio. Think specifically of what you would consider your Red Money. Do you know what is there? You may have several different investment products like individual mutual funds, bond accounts, stocks, etc. You may have inherited a stock portfolio from a relative, or you might be invested in a bond account offered by the company for which you worked due to your familiarity with them. While you may or may not be managing your investments individually, the reality is that you probably don't have an overall management strategy for all of your investments. Investments that aren't managed are simply Red Money, or money that is at risk in the market. Harnessing the earning potential of your Red Money relies on more than a collection of stocks and bonds, however. It needs guided management. A good Yellow Money manager uses the knowledge they have about the level of risk with which you are comfortable, what you need or want to use your money for, when you want or need it and how you want to use it. The Yellow Money objects that they choose for you will still have a certain level of risk, but under the right management, control and process, you have a far better chance of a successful outcome that meets your specific needs.

When you sit down with an investment professional, you can look at all of your assets together. Chances are that you have accumulated a number of different assets over the last 20, 30 or 50 years. You may have a 401(k), an IRA, a Roth IRA, an account of self-directed stocks, a brokerage account, etc. Wherever you put your money, a financial professional will go through your assets and help you determine the level of risk to which you are exposed now and should be exposed in the future.

Here is a typical example of how an investment professional can be helpful to a future retiree with Yellow Money needs:

» *Daisy is 65 years old and wants to retire in two years. She has a 401(k) from her job to which she has contributed for 26 years. She also has some stocks that her late husband managed. Daisy also has $55,000 in a mutual fund that her sister recommended to her five years ago and $30,000 in another mutual fund that she heard about at work. She takes a look at her assets one day and decides that she doesn't understand what they add up to or what kind of retirement they will provide. She decides to meet with an investment professional.*

Daisy's professional immediately asks her:

Does she know exactly where all of her money is? *Daisy doesn't know much about all her husband's stocks, which have now become hers. Their value is at $100,000 invested in three large cap companies. Daisy is unsure of the companies and whether she should hold or sell them.*

Does she know what types of assets she owns? *Yes and no. She knows she had a 401(k) and IRAs, but she is unfamiliar with her husband's self-directed stock portfolio or the type of mutual funds she owns. Furthermore she is unclear as to how to manage the holdings as she nears retirement.*

Does she know the strategies behind each one of the investment products she owns? *While Daisy knows she had a 401(k), an IRA and mutual fund holdings, she doesn't know how her 401(k) is organized or how to make it more conservative as she nears retirement. She is unsure whether her IRA is a Roth or traditional variety and how to draw income from them? She really does not have specific investment principles guiding her investment decisions, and she doesn't know anything about her husband's individual stocks. One major concern for Daisy is whether her family would be okay if she were not around?*

After determining Daisy's assets, her financial professional prepares a consolidated report that lays out all of her assets for

77

her to review. Her professional explains each one of them to her. Daisy discovers that although she is two years away from retiring, her 401(k) is organized with an amount of risk with which she is not comfortable. Sixty percent of her 401(k) is at risk, far off the mark if we abide by the Rule of 100. Daisy opts to be more conservative than the Rule of 100 suggests, as she will rely on her 401(k) for most of her immediate income needs after retirement. Daisy's professional also points out several instances of overlap between her mutual funds. Daisy learns that while she is comfortable with one of her mutual funds, she does not agree with the management principles of the other. In the end, Daisy's professional helps her re-organize her 401(k) to secure her more Green Money for retirement income. Her professional also uses her mutual fund and her husband's stock assets to create a growth oriented investment plan that Daisy will rely on for Need Later Money in 15 years when she plans on relocating closer to her children and grandchildren. By creating an overall investment strategy, Daisy is able to meet her targeted goals in retirement. Daisy's financial professional worked closely with her and her tax professional to minimize the tax impact of any asset sales on Daisy's situation.

Like Daisy, you may have several savings vehicles: a 401(k), an IRA to which you regularly contribute, some mutual funds to which you make monthly contributions, etc. But what is your *overall investment strategy?* Do you have one in place? Do you want one that will help you meet your retirement goals? Yellow Money looks at *ALL* your accounts and all their different strategies to create a plan that helps them all work together. Your current investment situation may not reflect your wishes. As a matter of fact, it likely doesn't.

You may have a better understanding of your assets than Daisy did, but even someone with an investment strategy can benefit from having a financial professional review their portfolio:

> » *Chad is 69 years old. He retired four years ago. He relied on income from an IRA for three years in order to increase his Social Security benefit. He also made significant investments in 36 different mutual funds. He chose to diversify among the funds by selecting a portion for growth, another for good dividends, another that focused on promising small cap companies and a final portion that work like index funds. All the money that Chad had in mutual funds he considered Need Later Money that he wanted to rely on in his 80s. After the stock market took a hit in 2008, Chad lost some confidence in his investments and decided to sit down with a financial professional to see if his portfolio was able to recover.*
>
> *The professional Chad met with was able to determine what goals he had in mind. Specifically, the financial professional determined what Chad actually wanted and needed the money for, and when he needed it. His professional also looked inside each of the mutual funds and discovered several instances of overlap. While Chad had created diversity in his portfolio by selecting funds focused on different goals, he didn't account for overlap in the companies in which the funds were invested. Out of the 36 funds, his professional found that 20 owned nearly identical stock. While most of the companies were good investments, the high instance of overlap did not contribute to the healthy investment diversity that Chad wanted. Chad's financial professional also provided him with a report that explained the concentration ratio of his holdings (noting how much of his portfolio was contained within the top 25 stock holdings), the percentage of his portfolio that each company in which he invested in represented (showing*

the percentage of net assets that each company made up as an overall position in his portfolio) and the portfolio date of his account (showing when the funds in his portfolio were last updated: as funds are required to report updates only twice per year, it was possible that some of his fund reports could be six months old).

Chad's professional consolidated his assets into one investment management strategy. This allowed Chad's investments to be managed by someone he trusted who knew his specific investment goals and needs. Eliminating redundancy and overlap in his portfolio was easy to do but difficult to detect since Chad had multiple funds with multiple brokerage firms. Chad sat down with a professional to see if his mutual funds could perform well, and he left with a consolidated management plan and a money manager that understood him personally. That's Yellow Money at its best.

FOLLOW YOUR HEAD: CREATING AN INVESTMENT STRATEGY

It's clear that when you make investment decisions using your emotions as your guide, financial calamity can easily follow. However, it's easy to make emotional investment decisions because it's easy to be emotional about your money. And, in some ways, why wouldn't you be? You've spent your life working for it, exchanging your time and talent for it, and making decisions about how to invest it, save it and make it grow. The maintenance of your lifestyle and your plans for retirement all depend on it. That said, however, the best investment strategies don't rely on emotions. One of Yellow Money's greatest strengths lies in the fact that it is managed by someone who understands your needs and desires, but doesn't make decisions about your money under the influence of emotion.

A well-managed investment account meets your goals as a whole, not in individualized and piecemeal ways. Professional money managers do this by creating requirements for each type of investment in which they put your money. We'll call them "screens." Your money manager will run your holdings through the screens they have created to evaluate different types of investment strategies. A professionally managed account will only have holdings that meet the requirements laid out in the overall management plan that was designed to meet your investment goals. The holdings that don't make it through the screens, the ones that don't contribute to your investment goals, are sold and redistributed to investments that your financial professional has determined to be appropriate.

Different screens apply to different Yellow Money strategies. For example, if one of your goals is significant growth, which would require taking on more risk alongside the potential for more return, an investment professional would screen for companies that have high rates of revenue and sales growth, high earnings growth, rising profit margins, and innovative products. On the other hand, if you want your portfolio to be used for income, which would call for lower risk and less return, your professional would screen for dividend yield and sector diversification. *Every investor has a different goal, and every goal requires a customized strategy that uses quantitative screens.* A professional will create a portfolio that reflects your investment desires. If some of the current assets you own complement the strategies that your professional recommends, those will likely stay in your portfolio.

Screening your assets removes emotions from the equation. It removes attachment to underperforming or overly risky investments. Financial professionals aren't married to particular stocks or mutual funds for any reason. They go by the numbers and see your portfolio through a lens shaped by your retirement goals. Your professional understands your wants and needs, and creates an investment strategy that takes your life events and future plans into account. It's a planful approach, and it allows you to tap into the tools and resources of a professional who has built a career around successful investing. Managing money is a full time job and is best left to a professional money manager.

Removing emotions from investing also allows you to be unaffected by the day-to-day volatility of the market. Your financial professional doesn't ask where the market is going to be in a year, three years or a month from now. If you look at the value of the stock market from the beginning of the twentieth century to today, it's going up. Despite the Great Depression, despite the 1987 crash, despite the 2008 market downturn, the market, as a whole, trends up. Remember the major market downturn in 2008 when the market lost 30 percent of its value? Not only did it completely recover, it has far exceeded its 2008 value. Emotional investing led countless people to sell low as the market went down, and buy the same shares back when the market started to recover. That's an expensive way to do business. While you can't afford to lose money that you need in two, three or five years, your Need Later Money has time to grow. The best way to do so is to make it Yellow and take a more managed investment approach tailored to your goals. Just like Daisy and Chad, chances are that by incorporating Yellow Money within your portfolio, you will have much to gain.

So what does a Yellow Money account look like? Here's what it *doesn't* look like: a portfolio with 49 small cap mutual funds, a dozen individual stocks and an assortment of bond accounts. A brokerage account with a hodgepodge of investments, even if goal-oriented, is not a professionally managed account. It's still Red Money. Remember, Yellow Money is a managed account that has an overarching investment philosophy. When you look at making investments that will perform to meet your future income needs, the burning question becomes: How much should you have in the market and how should it be invested? Working with a professional will help you determine how much risk you should take, how to balance your assets so they will meet your goals and how to plan for the big ticket items, like health care expenses, that may be in your future. Yes, Yellow Money is exposed to risk, but by working with a professional, you can manage that risk in a productive way.

WHY YELLOW MONEY?

If you have met your immediate income needs for retirement, why bother with professionally managing your other assets? The money you have accumulated above and beyond your income needs probably has a greater purpose. It may be for your children or grandchildren. You may want to give money to a charity or organization that you admire. In short, you may want to craft your legacy. It would be advantageous to grow your assets in the best manner possible. A financial professional has built a career around managing money in profitable ways. They are experts under the supervision of the organization that they represent.

Turning to Yellow Money also means that you don't have to burden yourself with the time commitment, the stress, and the cost of determining how to manage your money. Yellow Money can help you better enjoy your retirement. Do you want to sit down in your home office every day and determine how to best allocate your assets, or do you want to be living your life while someone else manages your money for you? When a financial professional manages the majority of your Red Money with a specific purpose, it frees you from having to worry about which stocks to buy and sell today and you can focus on your plans for tomorrow.

KNOWING WHERE TO TURN: SEEKING FINANCIAL ADVICE

When it comes to money, it can sometimes feel like everyone has an opinion about how it should be managed. However, even though financial advice is never hard to find, financial advice that is credible, sensible and affordable is much harder to come by. In order to increase your chances of finding the guidance you need to help you smoothly transition your Red Money into Yellow Money, it's important to understand that in today's investment world there are essentially two main places for you to look: with a stock broker and with an investment advisor. While these financial professionals have similar primary functions, the ways in which they perform them are incredibly different. To get an idea of how, consider this survey conducted by TD Ameritrade that shows the top reasons investors gave to explain their decision to work with an independent registered investment advisor:*

- Registered Investment Advisors are required, as fiduciaries, to offer advice that is in the best interest of clients
- More personalized service and competitive fee structure offered at a Registered Investment Advisor firm
- Dissatisfaction with full commission brokers

Of course, this list is not exhaustive by any means but it does highlight two crucial distinctions worth exploring further. First, a Registered Investment Advisor has no incentive to push clients towards products or strategies that pay the highest commissions because they are paid according to a fee structure. Secondly, and most importantly, Registered Investment Advisors are legally bound to always act in their client's best interest. These two factors, as well as the additional points outlined below, help to illustrate why Registered Investment Advisors make excellent vanguards for shifting your Red Money into Yellow Money:

- Investment advisor representatives have the fiduciary duty to act in a client's best interest at all times with every

---

2011 Advisor Sentiment Study, commissioned by TD AMERITRADE. TD Ameritrade, Inc.

investment decision they make. Stock brokers and broker-age firms usually do not act as fiduciaries to their investors and are not obligated to make decisions that are entirely in the best interest of their customers. For example, if you decide you want to invest in precious metals, a stock bro-ker would offer you a precious metals account from their firm. An Investment Advisor would find you a precious metals account that is the best fit for you based on the investment strategy of your portfolio.

- Investment advisors give their clients a Form ADV de-scribing the methods that the professional uses to do busi-ness. An Investment Advisor also obtains client consent regarding any conflicts of interest that could exist with the business of the professional.

- Stock brokers and brokerage firms are not obligated to provide comparable types of disclosure to their customers.

- Whereas stock brokers and firms routinely earn large profits by trading as principal with customers, Investment Advisors cannot trade with clients as principal (except in very limited and specific circumstances).

- Investment Advisors charge a pre-negotiated fee with their clients in advance of any transactions. They cannot earn additional profits or commissions from their customers' investments without prior consent. Registered Investment Advisors are commonly paid an asset-based fee that aligns their interests with those of their clients. Brokerage firms and stock brokers, on the other hand, have much different payment agreements. Their revenues may increase regard-less of the performance of their customers' assets.

- Unlike brokerage firms, where investment banking and underwriting are commonplace, Registered Investment Advisors must manage money in the best interests of their customers. Because Registered Investment Advisors charge set fees for their services, their focus is on their client. Brokerage firms may focus on other aspects of the firm that do not contribute to the improvement of their clients' assets.

- Unlike brokers, Registered Investment Advisors do not get commissions from fund or insurance companies for selling their investment products.

Just to drive home the point, here is what a fiduciary duty to a client means for a Registered Investment Advisor. Registered Investment Advisors must:*

- Always act in the best interest of their client and make investment decisions that reflect their goals.
- Identify and monitor securities that are illiquid.
- When appropriate, employ fair market valuation procedures.
- Observe procedures regarding the allocation of investment opportunities, including new issues and the aggregation of orders.
- Have policies regarding affiliated broker-dealers and maintenance of brokerage accounts.
- Disclose all conflicts of interest.
- Have policies on use of brokerage commissions for research.
- Have policies regarding directed brokerage, including step-out trades and payment for order flow.
- Abide by a code of ethics.

While there are a multitude of benefits that come from working with a Registered Investment Advisor, it's important to remember

---

2011 Advisor Sentiment Study, commissioned by TD AMERITRADE. TD Ameritrade, Inc.

that getting your affairs in order is a lengthy and multifaceted process that requires more than just financial planning for your retirement: it also necessitates tax planning, organizing your estate, developing a plan for long-term health care and creating a plan to transfer your assets. In other words, working with a Registered Investment Advisor will provide you with invaluable guidance and they will be a key player in the development of your plan but they will not be the only player.

Ultimately, when it comes to your Red Money, a Registered Investment Advisor plays a crucial in its management. However, as you know from the Rule of 100, the amount of money you have at risk should be reduced as you age, which means the importance of the role an RIA would play in your plan would be diminished. This is not to say that an RIA would no longer be necessary: rather, it simply means that there would be less for an RIA to do because your portfolio would consist of more Green Money than Red Money. Consequently, an RIA is not the only financial professional whose services are available to you: a seasoned financial advisor can also help by acting as the quarterback for your entire retirement plan. In other words, getting your affairs in order requires a myriad of different components and players to successfully integrate and work in concert with each other. This process often proves to be more involved than one single person can manage. Thus, it is frequently helpful to have another financial advisor, such as an estate planner, at the helm of your plan who can oversee its management and implementation. This will be addressed in more detail in later chapters.

|

CHAPTER 6 RECAP //

- When you put your Red Money into the hands of a professional it becomes Yellow Money and is not as dangerous.
- The success of your financial plan should not be contingent upon the performance of your Red Money. Your daily life should not be affected if your Red Money takes a beating in the market. This mindset will help you avoid emotional investing and to stay invested long enough to see some returns.
- Choosing the right financial professional to work with is one of the most important investment decisions you can make.

7

Thinking Outside the Box

New Ideas for Investing to Insure Your Future

As discussed earlier, the current economic climate represents a maelstrom of difficulties. From high market volatility to low interest rates, the path towards financial success and security is a rocky one. In order to overcome these obstacles, it's necessary to avoid using old and traditional patterns of financial thinking. The most familiar, and possibly most limiting, perspective to fall back on is framing investment through the old "risk versus reward" lens. With this viewpoint, investment opportunities are considered to exist solely along a sliding scale between risk and reward: the higher the exposure to volatility, the greater the return potential of the investment, while on the other hand, lower risk investments are accompanied by lower rates of return. For people who see all investments as the result of this trade-off, they often spend their financial lives sliding up and down this scale trying to strike a tolerable balance between risk and reward because according to this old investing rule, you can either choose relative safety *or* return, but you can't have both.

However, the utility of the outdated "risk versus reward" perspective can be drastically improved upon when you apply the concept of liquidity to expand its scope. The flexibility of liquidity helps to rewrite the old investment rules and create a broader financial lens through which you can craft the retirement plan that will be best suited to address your diverse needs. With this new perspective, there are essentially three dimensions that are inherent to any investment: *Liquidity, Safety,* and *Return.* You can maximize any two of these dimensions but always at the expense of the third. Keeping all your assets in a checking account or savings account, for example, is a financial decision that would maximize your Safety and Liquidity because you would be able to access your money whenever you wanted and it would not be exposed to any market volatility, but you would also sacrifice any opportunity for Return because the money would not be invested in a financial vehicle with any growth potential. Contrarily, if you selected Return and Liquidity as the two primary focal points of an investment, this decision would be made at the expense of the investment's Safety so your money would most likely be exposed to a very high level of risk.

Understanding Liquidity can help you break the old Risk versus Safety trade-off. The sooner you want your money back, the less you can leverage it for Safety or Return. If you have the option of putting your money in a long-term investment, you will be sacrificing Liquidity, but potentially gaining both Safety and Return. Ultimately, by identifying assets from which you don't require Liquidity, you can place yourself in a position to potentially profit from relatively safe investments that provide a higher than average rate of return.

LIQUIDITY AND RETIREMENT

Applying this three dimensional investment perspective can have a deep impact on all investment decisions but especially when it comes to retirement planning. In regards to retirement, it can be more useful to think of Safety as preservation, Return as accumulation, and Liquidity as income. Just as it is a mistake to frame general investment decisions as being only a trade-off between Safety and Return, it is equally as problematic to frame retirement decisions as primarily a trade-off between preservation and accumulation. As you've seen, your financial needs during retirement are complicated and satisfying them is not just a matter of figuring out an answer to the question, "how much money do I need to last my whole retirement and how can I acquire and protect it?" It's equally (if not more) important to answer the question of *when* you will need that money.

In other words, how much Liquidity do you *really* need? Think about it. If you haven't sat down and created an income plan for your retirement, your perceived need for Liquidity is a guess. You don't know how much cash you'll need to fill the income gap if you don't know the amount of your Social Security benefit or the total of your other income options. If you *have* determined your income need and have made a plan to fill your income gap, you can partition your assets based on when you will need them. Completing this exercise makes it much easier for you to see how you can apply new investment rules to get the most out of your assets, which is crucial given the uncertain and turbulent nature of today's economy. When you take into consideration such factors as inflation, market volatility, increasing taxation, fluctuating interest rates and other economic forces outside of our control, it becomes apparent why successful retirement plans attempt to find the most profitable and practical balance between your preservation, accumulation and income needs.

One of the hardest things about retirement planning is the financial mental shift it requires: the earning and saving paradigm that guided your financial life before retirement has to be replaced with an asset leveraging one. The shift will happen whether or not you're ready for it but utilizing the concept of Liquidity can help you prepare for this change. In Leon's case, the transition from earning and saving to leveraging assets was a costly one.

> » *Leon is a potato farmer with over 2,000 acres of land. Leon always tries to have somewhere between $50,000 and $90,000 in his checking and savings accounts because if an unexpected problem were to occur, Leon would need money readily available so he would be able to address the issue and carry on with farming. For example, if a crucial piece of equipment broke down, Leon would need to be able to pay for its repair or replacement as soon as possible. Similarly, if the price of pesticide were to increase, he would need to have enough money saved to compensate for the sudden increase in overhead to his business.*
>
> *As a farmer, most of Leon's wealth is tied up in his land and crops, which means when a major financial need arises, Leon can't just harvest more potatoes and use them as payment. In other words, the success of Leon's business depends on his ability to expect the unexpected and have enough money on hand in case calamity strikes and he needs cash quickly. Put another way, successfully farming requires that Leon maintain a certain amount of Liquidity and he gets used to keeping his saving account that well-stocked.*
>
> *When Leon retires, however, it never occurs to him that this habit was born of a necessity that no longer exists so he continues to keep the majority of his money in the bank. After selling most of his land and all of his equipment, Leon does what he always has and deposits the money into his saving ac-*

count. Unfortunately, this adherence to Liquidity means that Leon's assets aren't even keeping pace with inflation. After a lifetime of intense work and stress, the value of Leon's money is actually decreasing a little each day because he didn't adjust his financial perspective from earning and saving to leveraging his assets to accumulate value and generate income.

Almost anything would be a better option for Leon than clinging to Liquidity. He could have done something better to get either more return from his money or more safety, and at the very least would not have lost out to inflation.

Had Leon taken the time to organize his assets and create a purposeful plan for his retirement, he would have realized his adherence to the concept of Liquidity would be unnecessary and costly. Had Leon rethought his approach to money and had a better plan for retirement, he could have developed an investment strategy that would have helped him structure his assets in a way to both generate income and maintain some of their growth potential. As you know, there is no single investment tool or strategy that perfectly accomplishes this goal. However, having a broader investment perspective does allow you to consider options that might otherwise be overlooked: using life insurance is one such tool.

LIFE INSURANCE AND YOUR RETIREMENT

Life insurance is generally framed as a tool that is best suited for legacy planning and while its utility in this regard cannot be understated, it also has the potential to build wealth and be used as an investment vehicle that can be used to accumulate wealth and significantly enhance the strength and security of your retirement plan. Frequently, people consider life insurance's primary advantage to be its death benefit: the amount that your beneficiaries will receive after you have died so that they can pay your final expenses and to help them financially so they will be able to comfortably carry on with their lives without you. While it's true that there is no better way than life insurance to make sure that our loved ones will continue to be financially cared for and protected even after we are gone, the truth of the matter is that it is also an incredibly diverse tool that can be used to serve a variety of different financial functions.

However, the true utility of a life insurance policy runs much deeper than this ability for three main reasons: first and foremost, any money paid out by a life insurance policy will not be taxed, secondly, many policies carry within them a cash accumulation value, and finally, you can receive money from your life insurance while you're still alive through the use of policy loans. Consequently, not only can a life insurance policy be used for legacy planning, is also an invaluable instrument to have in your retirement planning toolbox.

To understand how this is possible, let's briefly look at how life insurance policies function, in general. There are two main classes of life insurance: **term** and **permanent**. Term life insurance is an idea with which most people are familiar. With term life insurance, you purchase a certain amount of death benefit that will go to your heirs upon your death but this policy will only be in effect for as long as the term of your policy, typically 10 to 20 years. Alternatively, permanent life insurance has no term involved. It will remain in effect throughout your entire life so long as you continue to pay the premiums. This option is often generally accompanied by higher premiums than term insurance for the same amount of death benefit coverage.

As a result of its higher initial cost, many people opt for term insurance and miss out on the benefits of permanent. However, there are significant differences between these two policies that are not often considered during a comparative analysis of the cost between the two policies. For example, it's important to keep in mind how often term life insurance policies actually pay out. Most often, term policies usually expire before the death of the policy-holder.

In fact, insurance studies show less than one percent of all term policies pay out death benefit claims. Consequently, if your term expires and you still want to have insurance you will have to purchase another policy, which could be an issue for several reasons. Not the least of which is that a term policy with the same benefit will be much more expensive than your original policy and, many times, health issues that occurred during the term of your previous policy, such as cancer or a heart condition, may make it impossible to acquire another policy. If this unfortunate event were to occur, your loved ones would be unprotected and you would lose out on all the potential legacy and retirement planning benefits provided by life insurance's tax-advantaged status.

THE LASTING BENEFITS OF PERMANENT LIFE INSURANCE

As we learned earlier through the discussion of annuities, insurance companies like predictability so they make long-term investments that will stabilize the amount of money they both pay out and receive. As a result, when you buy a permanent life insurance policy, the life insurance company will invest a certain portion of your premium and then pay interest on this amount. It is the increasing build up of this interest that accounts for the cash accumulation potential of your policy. Essentially, permanent life insurance policies have, in addition to its death benefit, a cash value or living benefit. The death benefit is the face value of your policy and is how much money your heirs will receive upon your death, whereas the living benefit is how much cash value or interest has accrued within your policy, which can be accessed while you're still alive.

In other words, not only does permanent life insurance ensure your family will always be protected regardless of any health changes that may arise but also through the continued payment of your premiums, the value of your policy actually increases. What's more is that so long as you gave the policy enough time for its cash value to accumulate, you could use policy loans to withdraw money from it regardless of your age. This means that under a permanent policy your policy's value will grow, while a term insurance policy's benefit will remain level. However, policy loans aren't the only way you could access your death benefit while you're still alive: if you purchased a permanent life insurance policy with an accelerated benefit rider you could be eligible to receive early payment of your death benefit if you had a terminal illness or other debilitating health issue. While the specifics would vary according to the terms of your policy, purchasing an accelerated benefit rider could allow your life insurance policy to possibly help address any long-term care needs that may arise in the future.

How much your permanent life insurance policy's value will grow depends on what kind of policy you purchase. The different ways in which the internal rate of return of a policy is determined is similar to that of an annuity: some policies will have a set rate of return (fixed), others will vary with the market (variable), and still others will offer a guaranteed minimum rate that will increase up to a certain cap if the market does well (indexed). Unlike many other financial vehicles, the money contained within your permanent life insurance policy is extremely liquid. For instance, traditional IRAs don't allow account withdrawals before the age of 59½ years old and taking money out of an annuity before its contract term is over means being hit with surrender penalties. That said, you cannot purchase a permanent life insurance policy and then immediately withdraw money from it. Typically, there is a waiting period in place that must elapse before you can withdraw money so enough time will pass for the cash value of your policy to increase.

One final and exceptionally attractive element of a permanent life insurance policy is that, unlike traditional retirement accounts, there are no contribution limits. However, there are parameters in place to prevent a life insurance policy's cash accumulation potential and tax-free benefit from being misused, which could allow the policy to act as a tax shelter. To prohibit this, the government created what's known as a Modified Endowment Contract or MEC: essentially, if a life insurance policy is overfunded it will become a MEC and then any money the policy-holder withdraws from it will be subject to taxation.

So why doesn't everyone have permanent life insurance? For one thing, the premiums associated with permanent life insurance are unavoidably higher than term life insurance because of the flexibility and cash accumulation value it does provide policy-holders. And as mentioned earlier, an additional part of the problem has to do with peoples' misconceptions. Permanent life insurance is generally misconceived as something that is very expensive for a wealth accumulation vehicle because there are mortality charges (fees for the death benefit) that detract from the available returns. Furthermore, those returns do not yield as much as the stock market over the long run. This is why many times you will hear the phrase "buy term and invest the rest," where "term" refers to term insurance and "the rest" refers to the difference between a permanent policy's higher premium and a term policy's lower premium for the same coverage. As the previous comparison of term and permanent life insurance illustrates, this is an incomplete picture of the issue. This is not to say that a permanent life insurance policy will always be preferable to a term life insurance policy: the needs of your particular situation should always be the ultimate determinant when you're trying to decide what tool or strategy to use.

The most important thing to remember is that every person will have different objectives when it comes to getting their affairs in order, which means there is no single way to go about it. Remember that it's not difficult to fall into the old habit of positioning every investment decision along a sliding scale where Safety is at one end and Return is at the other. While it's true that investments that offer greater returns are often exposed to more market volatility and risk, using the concept of Liquidity can help offset the extent to which this occurs and will help you avoid falling into limiting and outdated patterns of thinking. What's more, Liquidity will not only make it easier for you to make the mental shift from an earning and saving financial paradigm to an asset leveraging one, but it will also widen the scope of your financial options. Think about the unique requirements of your situation: What are your priorities? What does your income plan tell you about your future needs? The answers to these questions will vary according to your circumstance and personal preferences and you will have to decide the best way to address them.

CHAPTER 7 RECAP //

- New financial strategies consider every investment to be comprised of three main elements: Safety, Return, and Liquidity. Or, when it comes to retirement investment strategies, Safety can be thought of as preservation, Return as accumulation, and Liquidity as income.
- Because no single financial strategy or tool can maximize all three of these components simultaneously, the goal is to find the most beneficial balance between them.
- By utilizing the concept of Liquidity, you will have a broader financial scope through which you can frame your retirement, which will help you develop more innovative and customizable retirement strategies, such as using life insurance as a wealth accumulation tool.
- The benefits of life insurance extend far beyond simply providing a death benefit. Through the use of policy loans, permanent life insurance policies can be used to create an additional retirement income source or a "living benefit."
- There are two basic classes of life insurance: term and permanent. Term life insurance policies are only in effect for a specific length of time and have no cash accumulation value. On the other hand, permanent life insurance policies never expire, so long as the premiums continue to be paid and do have cash accumulation value.
- Any money paid out by a life insurance policy is untaxed.

8

Taxation Nation

Taxes play a starring role in the theater of retirement planning. Everyone is familiar with taxes (you've been paying them your entire working life), but not everyone is familiar with how to make tax planning a part of their retirement strategy.

Taxes are taxes, right? You'll pay them before retirement and you'll pay them during retirement. What's the difference? The truth is that a planful approach to taxes can help you save money, protect your assets and ensure that your legacy remains intact.

How can a tax form do all that? The answer lies in planning. *Tax planning* and *tax reporting* are two very different things. Most people only *report* their taxes. March rolls around, people pull out their 1040s or use TurboTax to enter their income and taxable assets, and ship it off to Uncle Sam at the IRS. If you use a CPA to report your taxes, you are essentially paying them to record history. You have the option of being proactive with your taxes and to plan for your future by making smart, informed decisions about how taxes affect your overall financial plan. Working with a financial professional who, along with a CPA, makes recommendations about your finances to you, will keep you looking forward instead of in the rearview mirror as you enter retirement.

TAXES AND RETIREMENT

When you retire, you move from the earning and accumulation phase of your life into the asset distribution phase of your life. For most people, that means relying on Social Security, a 401(k), an IRA, or a pension. Wherever you have put your Green Money for retirement, you are going to start relying on it to provide you with the income that once came as a paycheck. Most of these distributions will be considered income by the IRS and will be taxed as such. There are exceptions to that (not all of your Social Security income is taxed, and income from Roth IRAs is not taxed), but for the most part, your distributions will be subject to income taxes.

Regarding assets that you have in an IRA or a 401(k) plan that uses an IRA, when you reach 70 ½ years of age, you will be required to draw a certain amount of money from your IRA as income each year. That amount depends on your age and the balance in your IRA. The amount that you are required to withdraw as income is called a Required Minimum Distribution (RMD). Why are you required to withdraw money from your own account? Chances are the money in that account has grown over time, and the government wants to collect taxes on that growth. If you have a large balance in an IRA, there's a chance your RMD could increase your income significantly enough to put you into a higher tax bracket, subjecting you to a higher tax rate.

Here's where tax planning can really begin to work strongly in your favor. In the distribution phase of your life, you have a predictable income based on your RMDs, your Social Security benefit and any other income-generating assets you may have. What really impacts you at this stage is how much of that money you keep in your pocket after taxes. Essentially, **you will make more money saving on taxes than you will by making more money.** If you can reduce your tax burden by 30, 20 or even 10 percent, you earn yourself that much more money by not paying it in taxes.

How do you save money on taxes? By having a plan. In this instance, a financial professional can work with the CPAs at their firm to create a **distribution plan** that minimizes your taxes and maximizes your annual net income.

BUILDING A TAX DIVERSIFIED PORTFOLIO

So far so good: avoid taxes, maximize your net annual income and have a plan for doing it. When people decide to leverage the experience and resources of a financial professional, they may not be thinking of how distribution planning and tax planning will benefit their portfolios. Often more exciting prospects like planning income annuities, investing in the market and structuring investments for growth rule the day. Taxes, however, play a crucial role in retirement planning. Achieving those tax goals requires knowledge of options, foresight and professional guidance.

Finding the path to a good tax plan isn't always a simple task. Every tax return you file is different from the one before it because things constantly change. Your expenses change. Planned or unplanned purchases occur. Health care costs, medical bills, an inheritance, property purchases, reaching an age where your RMD kicks in or travel, any number of things can affect how much income you report and how many deductions you take each year.

Preparing for the ever-changing landscape of your financial life requires a tax-diversified portfolio that can be leveraged to balance the incomes, expenditures and deductions that affect you each year. A financial professional will work with you to answer questions like these:

- What does your tax landscape look like?
- Do you have a tax-diversified portfolio robust enough to adapt to your needs?
- Do you have a diversity of taxable and non-taxable income planned for your retirement?
- Will you be able to maximize your distributions to take advantage of your deductions when you retire?
- Is your portfolio strong enough and tax-diversified enough to adapt to an ever-changing (and usually increasing) tax code?

» *When Marlene returns home after a week in the hospital recovering from a knee replacement, the 77-year-old calls her daughter, sister and brother to let them know she is home and feeling well. She also should have called her CPA. Marlene's medical expenses for the procedure, her hospital stay, her medications and the ongoing physical therapy she attended amount to more than $50,000.*

Currently, Americans can deduct medical expenses that are more than 7.5 percent of their Adjusted Gross Income (AGI). Marlene's AGI is $60,000 the year of her knee replacement, meaning she is able to deduct $44,000 of her medical bills from her taxes that year. Her AGI dictated that she could deduct more than 80 percent of her medical expenses that year. **Marlene didn't know this.**

Had she been working with a financial professional who regularly asked her about any changes in her life, her spending, or her expenses (expected or unexpected), Marlene could have saved thousands of dollars. Marlene can also file an amendment to her tax return to recoup the overpayment.

This relatively simple example of how tax planning can save you money is just the tip of the iceberg. No one can be expected to know the entire U.S. tax code. But an individual who is working with a team of CPAs and other financial professionals has an advantage over the average taxpayer who must start from square one on their own every year. Have you been taking advantage of all the deductions that are available to you?

PROACTIVE TAX PLANNING

The implications of proactive tax planning are far reaching, and are larger than many people realize. Remember, doing your taxes in January, February, March or April means you are writing a history book. Planning your taxes in October, November or December means that you are writing the story as it happens. You can look at all the factors that are at play and make decisions that will impact your tax return *before* you file it.

Realizing that tax planning is an aspect of financial planning is an important leap to make. When you incorporate tax planning into your financial planning strategy, it becomes part of the way you maximize your financial potential. Paying less in taxes means you keep more of your money. Simply put, the more money you keep, the more of it you can leverage as an asset. This kind of planning can affect you at any stage of your life. If you are 40 years old, are you contributing the maximum amount to your 401(k) plan? Are you contributing to a Roth IRA? Are you finding ways to structure the savings you are dedicating to your children's education? Do you have life insurance? Taxes and tax planning affects all of these investment tools. Having a relationship with a professional who works with a CPA can help you build a truly comprehensive financial plan that not only works with your investments, but also shapes your assets to find the most efficient ways to prepare for tax time. There may be years that you could benefit from higher distributions because of the tax bracket that you are in, or there could be years you would benefit from taking less. There may be years when you have a lot of deductions and years you have relatively few. **Adapting your distributions to work in concert with your available deductions** is at the heart of smart tax planning. Professional guidance can bring you to the next level of income distribution, allowing you to remain flexible enough to maximize your tax efficiency. And remember, saving money on taxes makes you more money than making money does.

What you have on paper is important: your assets, savings, investments, which are financial expression of your work and time. It's just as important to know how to get it off the paper in a way that keeps most of it in your pocket. Almost anything that involves financial planning also involves taxes. Annuities, investments, IRAs, 401(k)s, 403(b), and many other investment options will have tax implications. Life also has a way of throwing curveballs. Illness, expensive car repair or replacement, or *any event that has a financial impact on your life will likely have a corresponding tax implication* around which you should adapt your financial plan. Tax planning does just that.

One dollar can end up being less than 25 cents to your heirs.

> » *When Tim's father passed away, he discovered that he was the beneficiary of his father's $500,000 IRA. Tim has a wife and a family of four children, and he knew that his father had intended for a large portion of the IRA to go toward funding their college educations.*
>
> *After Tim's father's estate is distributed, Tim, who is 50 years old and whose two oldest sons are entering college, liquidates the IRA. By doing so, his taxable income for that year puts him in a 39.6 percent tax bracket, immediately reducing the value of the asset to $302,000. An additional 3.8 percent surtax on net investment income further diminishes the funds*

to $283,000. Liquidating the IRA in effect subjects much of Tim's regular income to the surtax, as well. At this point, Tim will be taxed at 43.4 percent.

Tim's state taxes are an additional 9 percent. Moreover, estate taxes on Tim's father's assets claim another 22 percent. By the time the IRS is through, Tim's income from the IRA will be taxed at 75 percent, leaving him with $125,000 of the original $500,000. While it would help contribute to the education of his children, it wouldn't come anywhere near completely paying for it, something the $500,000 could have easily done.

As the above example makes clear, leaving an asset to your beneficiaries can be more complicated than it may seem. In the case of a traditional IRA, after federal, estate and state taxes, the asset could literally diminish to as little as 25 percent of its value.

How does working with a professional help you make smarter tax decisions with your own finances? Any financial professional worth their salt will be working with a firm that has a team of trained tax professionals, including CPAs, who have an intimate knowledge of the tax code and how to adapt a financial plan to it.

Here's another example of how taxes have major implications on asset management:

» Howard and Caroline, a 62-year-old couple, begin working with a financial professional in October. After structuring their assets to reflect their risk tolerance and creating assets that would provide them Green Money income during retirement, they feel good about their situation. They make decisions that allow them to maximize their Social Security benefits, they have plenty of options for filling their income gap, and have begun a safe yet ambitious Yellow Money strategy with their professional. When their professional asks them about their

tax plan, they tell him their CPA handled their taxes every year, and did a great job. Their professional says, "I don't mean who does your taxes, I mean, who does your tax planning?" Howard and Caroline aren't sure how to respond.

Their professional brings Howard and Caroline's financial plan to the firm's CPA and has her run a tax projection for them. A week later their professional calls them with a tax plan for the year that will save them more than $3,000 on their tax return. The couple is shocked. A simple piece of advice from the CPA based on the numbers revealed that if they paid their estimated taxes before the end of the year, they would be able to itemize it as a deduction, allowing them to save thousands of dollars.

This solution won't work for everyone, and it may not work for Howard and Caroline every year. That's not the point. By being proactive with their approach to taxes and using the resources made available by their financial professional, they were able to create a tax plan that saved them money.

YELLOW MONEY AND TAXES

There are also tax implications for the money that you have managed professionally. People with portions of their investment portfolio that are actively traded can particularly benefit from having a proactive tax strategy. Without going into too much detail, for tax purposes there are two kinds of investment money: qualified and non-qualified. Different investment strategies can have different effects on how you are taxed on your investments and the growth of your investments. Some are more beneficial for one kind of investment strategy over another. Determining how to plan for the taxation of non-qualified and qualified investments is fodder for holiday party discussions at accounting firms. While it may not be a stimulating topic for the average investor, you don't have to understand exactly how it works in order to benefit from it.

While there are many differences between qualified and non-qualified investments, the main difference is this: qualified plans are designed to give investors tax benefits by deferring taxation of their growth until they are withdrawn. Non-qualified investments are not eligible for these deferral benefits. As such, non-qualified investments are taxed whenever income is realized from them in the form of growth.

Actively and non-actively traded investments provide a simple example of how to position your investments for the best tax advantage. In an actively traded and managed portfolio, there is a high amount of buying and selling of stocks, bonds, funds, ETFs, etc. If that active portfolio of non-qualified investments does well and makes a 20 percent return one year and you are in the 39.6 percent tax bracket, your net gain from that portfolio is only about 12 percent (39.6 percent tax of the 20 percent gain is roughly 8 percent.) In a passive trading strategy, you can use a qualified investment tool, such as an IRA, to achieve 13, 14 or 15 percent growth (much lower than the actively traded portfolio), but still realize a higher net return because the growth of the qualified investment is not taxed until it is withdrawn.

Does this mean that you have to always rely on a buy and hold strategy in qualified investment tools? Not necessarily. The question is, if you have qualified and non-qualified investments, where do you want to position your actively traded and managed assets? Incorporating a planful approach to positioning your investments for more beneficial taxation can be done many ways, but let's consider one example. Keeping your actively managed investment strategies inside an IRA or some other qualified plan could allow you to realize the higher gains of those investments without paying tax on their growth every year. Your more passively managed funds could then be kept in taxable, non-qualified vehicles and methods, and because you aren't realizing income from them on an annual basis by frequently trading them, they grow sheltered from taxation.

If you are interested in taking advantage of tax strategies that maximize your net income, you need the attentive strategies, experience and knowledge of a professional who can give you options that position you for profit. At the end of the day, what's important to you as the consumer is how much you keep, your after-tax take home.

ESTATE TAXES

The government doesn't just tax your income from investments while you're alive. They will also dip into your legacy.

While estate taxes aren't as hot of a topic as they were a few years ago, they are still an issue of concern for many people with assets. While taxes may not apply on estates that are less than $5 million, certain states have estate taxes with much lower exclusion ratios. Some are as low as $600,000. Many people may have to pay a state estate tax. One strategy for avoiding those types of taxes is to move assets outside of your estate. That can include gifting them to family or friends, or putting them into an irrevocable trust. Life insurance is another option for protecting your legacy.

CHAPTER 8 RECAP //

- Taxes are an inescapable fact of life. However, if you plan your taxes instead of just reporting them, you can mitigate the severity of their impact.
- After you have retired, saving money on taxes will provide you with more money than actually trying to make more money could provide. This is why you should develop a tax strategy that minimizes your taxation and therefore maximizes your income.

9

A Taxing Future

Tax legislation over the course of American history has left one very resounding message: taxes go up. Sadly, we hear this same threat so often that it has begun to sound like the boy who cried wolf. The reason behind this lies in the fact that tax hikes usually do not take effect until two or three years after their introduction and subsequently get piecemeal implementation. The result of this prolonged implementation period can be equated to death by a thousand paper cuts.

DEBT CEILING – CAUSE AND EFFECTS
The raising of the debt ceiling raised more than just the ability for our government to go further into debt. It also raised concerns and fears about the future of our economy. We are now seeing major swings in the markets with investors showing serious concerns over the future of investment valuations and their personal

wealth. Unfortunately, the reasoning behind all of this uncertainty is preceded by the inability to see the full implications of what is in store. We rarely talk about the fact that the discussions on raising the debt ceiling were coupled to discussions on major tax reforms needed to correct the problems underlining the debt ceiling increase itself.

Increasing the debt ceiling was needed because the government maxed out its credit card, so to speak, which it has been living off of for quite some time. It is really not much different than what we have been seeing from the general public for the past few decades. Unfortunately, most of us do not have the ability to get a credit limit increase on our credit cards once we reach the maximum limit, that is unless we can show the ability to pay this balance back. The only way to pay this credit card back is by spending less and making more money.

This is exactly where the federal government is today. They have been given a higher credit limit, but they still must find a way to decrease the spending while making more money. The only way the government makes money is by collecting taxes.

Unfortunately, at the current moment, the government is collecting approximately $120 billion less per month than it currently spends. Discussions for major tax reform have accompanied the discussions for the increased debt ceiling.

DEBT AND EARNINGS

Let us take a closer look at where we are today. The U.S. national debt is increasing at an alarming rate, rising to levels never seen before and threatening serious harm to the economy. Through the end of 2010, the national debt has risen to $13.6 trillion, averaging an 11.4 percent increase annually over the past five years and a 9.2 percent increase annually over the past 10 years. To put this into perspective, the national gross domestic product (GDP) has increased to $14.5 trillion during the same period, averaging a 2.9

percent annual increase over the past five years and a 3.9 percent increase over the past 10 years. At the end of 2010, the national debt level was 93 percent of the GDP. Economists believe that a sustainable economy exists at a maximum level of approximately 80 percent. As of December 20, 2013, the U.S. national debt is 107.69 percent of GDP with the debt at $17.252 trillion and the GDP at $16.020 trillion.*

The significance of these two numbers lies within the contrast. The national debt is the amount that needs to be repaid. This is the credit card balance. Gross domestic product on the other hand is less known and represents the market value of all final goods and services produced within a country during a given period. Essentially, GDP represents the gross taxable income available to the government. If debts are increasing at a greater rate than the gross income available for taxation, then the only way to make up the difference is by increasing the rate at which the gross income is taxed.

The most recent presidential budget shows a continuing trend in the disparity between growth in the national debt and GDP over the next two decades. Although the increasing disparity is a real concern and shows that, at least in the short run, the federal deficit will not be addressed to counteract the potential crisis ahead, it is the revenue collection that tells the disconcerting story. Over the past 40 years the average collection of GDP has been approximately 17.6 percent and currently collections are at approximately 14.4 percent of GDP.

As the presidential budget reveals, the projected revenues are estimated to be 20 percent by the end of the next decade. That is a 38.8 percent increase from the current tax levels. To put this into perspective, if you are currently in the top tax bracket of 35 percent and this bracket increases by the proposed collection

---

http://www.usdebtclock.org/12/20/13

increase, your tax rate will be approximately 48.5 percent. Keep in mind that even at this rate the deficit is projected to increase.

2013 – THE END OF AN ERA?

From a historical point of view, taxes are extremely low. The last time the U.S. national debt was at the same percentage level of GDP as today was at the end of World War II and several years following. The maximum tax rate averaged 90 percent from 1944 through 1963. Compare that to the maximum rate of 35 percent today and it becomes very clear that there is a disparity of extreme proportion.

Taxes during this historical period were at extreme levels for nearly 20 years, during and following this current level of debt-to-GDP. A significant point to note about the difference between that time and today is the economic activity. The period of 1944 through 1963 was in the heart of both the industrial revolution and the birth of the Baby Boom generation. Today, we are mired in extreme volatility with frequent periods of boom and bust at the same time we are witnessing the beginning of the greatest retirement wave ever experienced within the U.S. economy.

To contrast these two time periods in respect to the recovery period is almost asinine as the external pressures from globalization and domestic unfunded liabilities did not exist or were irrelevant factors during the prior period.

To add insult to injury, U.S. domestic unfunded liabilities are currently estimated somewhere around $61.6 trillion due to items such as Social Security, Medicare and government pensions. The most concerning part of this pertains to the coming wave of retirement as the Baby Boom generation begins retiring and drawing on the unfunded Social Security for which they currently have entitlement. Over the long run, expenditures related to healthcare programs such as Medicare and Medicaid are projected to grow faster than the economy overall as the population matures.

To put unfunded liabilities into perspective, consider these as off-balance-sheet obligations similar to those of Enron. Although these are not listed as part of the national debt, they must be paid. These liabilities exist outside of the annual budgetary debt discussed. The difference between Enron and the U.S. unfunded liabilities is that if the U.S. government cannot come up with the funds to pay all these liabilities through revenue generation, they will print the money necessary to pay the debt.

WHAT DOES THE SOLUTION LOOK LIKE?

Unfortunately, the general public is in a no-win situation for this solution to the problem. Printing money does not bode well for economic growth. This creates inflationary pressures that devalue the U.S. dollar and make everyone less wealthy. Cutting the entitlements that compose this liability leaves millions of people without benefits they have come to expect. The only other option, and one that the government knows all too well, is increasing taxes. In fact, according to a Congressional Budget Office paper issued in 2004:

"The term 'unfunded liability' has been used to refer to a gap between the government's projected financial commitment under a particular program and the revenues that are expected to be available to fund that commitment. But no government obligation can be truly considered 'unfunded' because of the U.S. government's sovereign power to tax—which is the ultimate resource to meet its obligations."

A balanced budget will be required at some point and with this will come higher taxes. We have uncertainty surrounding tax rates and how high they will go. At that time, extensions put in place in December 2010 on Bush-era tax cuts are set to expire. We are likely to see some tax increases at this point. Whether it is only on the top earners or unilaterally across all income levels is yet to be seen, but an increase of some sort will most certainly occur.

How do you prepare? Why spend so much time reassuring you that taxes will increase? Because you have an opportunity to take action. Now is the time to prepare for what will come and structure countermeasures for the good, the bad and the ugly of each of these legislative nightmares through tax-advantaged retirement planning.

You make more money by saving on taxes than you do by making more money. The simplistic logic of the statement makes sense when you discover it takes $1.50 in earnings to put that same dollar, saved in taxes, back in your pocket.

As simple as it sounds, it is much more difficult to execute. Most people fail to put together a plan as they near retirement, beginning with a simple cash flow budget. If you have not analyzed your proposed income streams and expenses, you could not possibly have taken the time to position these cash flows and other events into a tax-preferred plan.

Most people will state that they have a plan and, thus, do not need any further assistance in this area. The truth in most instances is that people could not show you their plan, and among the few that could, most would not be able to show you how they have executed it. In this regard, they might as well be Richard Nixon stating, "I am not a crook" for as much as they state, "I have a plan." The truth lies in waiting. As we approach or begin retirement, we should look at what cash flows we will have. Do we have a pension? How about Social Security? How much additional cash flow am I going to need to draw from my assets to maintain the lifestyle that I desire?

We spend our whole lives saving and accumulating wealth but spend so little time determining how to distribute this accumulation so as to retain it. We need to make sure we have the appropriate diversification of taxable versus non-taxable assets to complement our distribution strategy.

THE BENEFITS OF DIVERSIFICATION

Heading into retirement, we should be situated with a diversified tax landscape. The point to spending our whole lives accumulating wealth is not to see the size of the number on paper, but rather to be an exercise in how much we put in our pocket after removing it from the paper. To truly understand tax diversification, we must understand what types of money exist and how each of these will be treated during accumulation and, most importantly, during distribution. The following is a brief summary:

1. Free money
2. Tax-advantaged money
3. Tax-deferred money
4. Taxable money
   a. Ordinary income
   b. Capital gains and qualified dividends

FREE MONEY

Free money is the best kind of money regardless of tax treatment because, in the end, you have more money than you would have otherwise. Many employers will provide contributions toward employee retirement accounts to offer additional employment benefits and encourage employees to save for their own retirement. With this, employers often will offer a matching contribution in which they contribute up to a certain percentage of an employee's salary (generally three to five percent) toward that employee's retirement account when the employee contributes to their retirement account as well. For example, if an employee earns $50,000 annually and contributes three percent ($1,500) to their retirement account annually, the employer will also contribute three percent ($1,500) to the employee's account. That is $1,500 in free money. Take all you can get! Bear in mind that any employer contribution to a 401(k) will still be subject to taxation when withdrawn.

TAX-ADVANTAGED MONEY

Tax-advantaged money is the next best thing to free money. Although you have to earn tax-advantaged money, you do not have to give part of it away to Uncle Sam. Tax-advantaged money comes in three basic forms that you can utilize during your lifetime; four if prison inspires your future, but we are not going to discuss that option.

One of the most commonly known forms of tax-advantaged money is municipal bonds, which earn and pay interest that could be tax-advantaged on the federal level, or state level, or both. There are several caveats that should be discussed with regard to the notion of tax-advantaged income from municipal bonds. First, you will notice that tax-advantaged has several flavors from the state and federal perspective. This is because states will generally tax the interest earned on a municipal bond unless the bond is offered from an entity located within that state. This severely limits the availability of completely tax-advantaged municipal bonds and constrains underlying risk and liquidity factors. Second, municipal bond interest is added back into the equation for determining your modified adjusted gross income (MAGI) for Social Security. This could push your income above a threshold and subject a portion of your Social Security income to taxation.

In effect, if this interest subjects some other income to taxation then this interest is truly being taxed.

Last, municipal bond interest may be excluded from the regular federal tax system, but it is included for determining tax under the alternative minimum tax (AMT) system. In its basic form, the AMT system is a separate tax system that applies if the tax computed under AMT exceeds the tax computed under the regular tax system. The difference between these two computations is the alternative minimum tax.

TAX-ADVANTAGED MONEY: ROTH IRA

Roth accounts are probably the single greatest tax asset that has come from Congress outside of life insurance. They are well known but rarely used. Roth IRAs were first established by the Taxpayer Relief Act of 1997 and named after Senator William Roth, the chief sponsor of the legislation. Roth accounts are simply an account in the form of an individual retirement account or an employer sponsored retirement account that allows for tax-advantaged growth of earnings and, thus, tax-advantaged income.

The main difference between a Roth and a traditional IRA or employer-sponsored plan lies in the timing of the taxation. We are all very familiar with the typical scenario of putting money away for retirement through an employer plan, whereby they deduct money from our paychecks and put it directly into a retirement account. This money is taken out before taxes are calculated, meaning we do not pay tax on those earnings today. A Roth account, on the other hand, takes the money after the taxes have been removed and puts it into the retirement account, so we do pay tax on the money today. The other significant difference between these two is taxation during distribution in later years. Regarding our traditional retirement accounts, when we take the money out later it is added to our ordinary income and is taxed accordingly. Additionally, including this in our income subjects us to the consequences mentioned above for municipal bonds with Social Security taxation, AMT, as well as higher Medicare premiums. A Roth on the other hand is distributed tax-advantaged and does not contribute toward negative impact items such as Social Security taxation, AMT, or Medicare premium increases. It essentially comes back to us without tax and other obligations.

The best way to view the difference between the two accounts is to look at the life of a farmer. A farmer will buy seed, plant it in the ground, grow the crops and harvest it later for sale. Typically, the farmer would only pay tax on the crops that have been harvested and sold. But if you were the farmer, would you rather pay tax on the $5,000 of seed that you plant today or the $50,000 of crops harvested later? The obvious answer is $5,000 of seed today. The truth to the matter is that you are a farmer, except you plant dollars into your retirement account instead of seeds into the earth.

So why doesn't everyone have a Roth retirement account if things are so simple? There are several reasons, but the single greatest reason has been the constraints on contributions. If you earned over certain thresholds (MAGI over $125,000 single and $183,000 joint for 2012), you were not eligible to make contributions, and until last year, if your modified adjusted gross income (MAGI) was over $100,000 (single or joint), you could not convert a traditional IRA to a Roth. Outside these contribution limits, most people save for retirement through their employers and most employers do not offer Roth options in their plans. The reason behind this is because Roth accounts are not that well understood and people have been educated to believe that saving on taxes today is the best possible course of action.

TAX-ADVANTAGED MONEY: LIFE INSURANCE

As you learned previously, money paid out by a life insurance policy is not taxed, which makes life insurance the most significant tax asset to have ever been created by Congress. Life insurance is the little-known or little-discussed tax asset that holds some of the greatest value in your financial history both during life and upon death. Regardless of what type of life insurance policy you purchase, no one has to pay taxes on any money received from it, which makes it the best tax-advantaged device available by far. For example, if your life insurance policy is used only as a legacy-planning tool, the death benefit your heirs receive will not be taxed, nor will it effect the taxation of their other assets in any way. Likewise, if you purchased a permanent life insurance policy so its cash accumulation potential could be harnessed to allow it to function as a retirement planning tool, any income generated by the policy would also be tax-free.

The utility of life insurance's tax-free nature cannot be understated: of the three phases of retirement planning (contribution, distribution, and transfer), only the contribution stage is subjected to taxation, which allows the funds within a permanent life insurance policy to grow tax-free, be withdrawn tax-free, and be transferred to beneficiaries tax-free. Thus, even though life insurance is typically only thought of as having a "death benefit," it can also be designed to function as a living benefit if it is structured properly.

TAX-DEFERRED MONEY

Tax-deferred money is the type of money with which most of people are familiar, but we also briefly reviewed the idea above. Tax-deferred money is typically our traditional IRA, employer sponsored retirement plan or a non-qualified annuity. Essentially, you put money into an investment vehicle that will accumulate in value over time and you do not pay taxes on the earnings that grow these accounts until you distribute them. Once the money is distributed, taxes must be paid. However, the same negative consequences exist with regard to additional taxation and expense in other areas as previously discussed. The cash accumulation value can be used for tax-advantaged income.

TAXABLE MONEY

Taxable money is everything else and is taxable today, later or whenever it is received. These four types of money come down to two distinct classifications: taxable and tax-free. The greatest difference when comparing taxable and tax-advantaged income is a function of how much money we keep after tax. For help in determining what the differences should be, excluding outside factors such as Social Security taxation and AMT, a tax equivalent yield should be used.

TAX-ADVANTAGED IN THE REAL WORLD

To put the tax equivalent yield into perspective, let us look at an example: Bob and Mary are currently retired, living on Social Security and interest from investments and falling within the 25 percent tax bracket. They have a substantial portion of their investments in municipal bonds yielding 6 percent, which is quite comforting in today's market. The tax equivalent yield they would need to earn from a taxable investment would be 8 percent, a 2 percent gap that seems almost impossible given current market volatility. However, something that has never been put into perspective is that the interest from their municipal bonds is subject to taxation on their Social Security benefits (at 21.25 percent). With this, the yield on their municipal bonds would be 4.725 percent, and the taxable equivalent yield falls to 6.3 percent, leaving a gap of only 1.575 percent.

In the end, most people spend their lives accumulating wealth through the best, if not the only vehicle they know, a tax-deferred account. This account is most likely a 401(k) or 403(b) plan offered through our employer and may be supplemented with an IRA that was established at one point or another. As the years go by, people blindly throw money into these accounts in an effort to save for a retirement that we someday hope to reach.

The truth is, most people have an age selected for when they would like to retire, but spend their lives wondering if they will ever be able to actually quit working. To answer this question, you must understand how much money you will have available to contribute toward your needs. ***In other words, you need to know what your after-tax income will be during this period.***

All else being equal, it would not matter if you put your money into a taxable, tax-deferred or tax-advantaged account as long as income tax rates never change and outside factors are never an event. The net amount you receive in the end will be the same.

Unfortunately, this will never be the case. We already know that taxes will increase in the future, meaning we will likely see higher taxes in retirement than during our peak earning years.

Regardless, saving for retirement in any form is a good thing as it appears from all practical perspectives that future government benefits will be cut and taxes will increase. You have the ability to plan today for efficient tax diversification and maximization of our after-tax dollars during your distribution years.

CHAPTER 9 RECAP //

- Taxes are how the government generates income for itself.
- There are two things you can count on: you will always have to pay taxes and our current debt crisis indicates our taxes are only going to get higher.
- There are four kinds of money: free money, tax-advantaged money, tax-deferred money, and taxable money.

10

Choosing a Bridge: The Brandeis Story

Louis Brandeis provides one of the best examples illustrating how tax planning works. Brandeis was Associate Justice on the Supreme Court of the United States from 1916 to 1939. Born in Louisville, Kentucky, Brandeis was an intelligent man with a touch of country charm. He described tax planning this way:

"I live in Alexandria, Virginia. Near the Court Chambers, there is a toll bridge across the Potomac. When in a rush, I pay the dollar toll and get home early. However, I usually drive outside the downtown section of the city and cross the Potomac on a free bridge.

The bridge was placed outside the downtown Washington, D.C. area to serve a useful social service—getting drivers to drive the extra mile and help alleviate congestion during the rush hour.

If I went over the toll bridge and through the barrier without paying a toll, I would be committing tax evasion.

If I drive the extra mile and drive outside the city of Washington to the free bridge, I am using a legitimate, logical and suitable method of tax avoidance, and I am performing a useful social service by doing so.

*The tragedy is that **few people know that the free bridge exists.** "*

Like Brandeis, most American taxpayers have options when it comes to "crossing the Potomac," so to speak. It's a financial planner's job to tell you what options are available. You can wait until March to file your taxes, at which time you might pay someone to report and pay the government a larger portion of your income. However, you could instead file before the end of the year, work with your financial professional and incorporate a tax plan as part of your overall financial planning strategy. Filing later is like crossing the toll bridge. Tax planning is like crossing the free bridge.

Which would you rather do?

The answer to this question is easy. Most people want to save money and pay less in taxes. What makes this situation really difficult in real life, however, is that the signs along the side of the road that direct us to the free bridge are not that clear. To normal Americans, and to plenty of people who have studied it, the U.S. tax code is easy to get lost in. There are all kinds of rules, exceptions to rules, caveats and conditions that are difficult to understand, or even to know about. What you really need to know is your options and the bottom line impacts of those options.

ROTH IRA CONVERSIONS

The attractive qualities of Roth IRAs may have prompted you to explore the possibility of moving some of your assets into a Roth account. Another important difference between the accounts is how they treat Required Minimum Distributions (RMDs). When you turn 70 ½ years old, you are required to take a minimum amount of money out of a traditional IRA. This amount is your RMD. It is treated as taxable income. Roth IRAs, however, do not have RMDs, and their distributions are not taxable. Quite a deal, right?

While having a Roth IRA as part of your portfolio is a good idea, converting assets to a Roth IRA can pose some challenges, depending on what kinds of assets you want to transfer.

One common option is the conversion of a traditional IRA to a Roth IRA. You may have heard about converting your IRA to a Roth IRA, but you might not know the full net result on your income. The main difference between the two accounts is that the growth of investments within a traditional IRA is not taxed until income is withdrawn from the account, whereas taxes are charged on contribution amounts to a Roth IRA, not withdrawals. The problem, however, is that when assets are removed from a traditional IRA, even if the assets are being transferred to a Roth IRA account, taxes apply.

There are a lot of reasons to look at Roth conversions. People have a lot of money in IRAs, up to multiple millions of dollars. Even with $500,000, when they turn 70 ½ years old, their RMD is going to be approximately $18,000, and they have to take that out whether they want to or not. It's a tax issue. Essentially, if you will be subject to high RMDs, it could have impacts on how much of your Social Security is taxable, and on your tax bracket.

By paying taxes now instead of later on assets in a Roth IRA, you can realize tax-advantaged growth. You pay once and you're done paying. Your heirs are done paying. It's a powerful tool. Here's a simple example to show you how powerful it can be:

Imagine that you pay to convert a traditional IRA to a Roth. You have decided that you want to put the money in a vehicle that gives you a tax-advantaged income option down the road. If you pay a

25 percent tax on that conversion and the Roth IRA then doubles in value over the next 10 years, you could look at your situation as only having paid 12.5 percent tax.

The prospect of tax-advantaged income is a tempting one. While you have to pay a conversion tax to transfer your assets, you also have turned taxable income into tax free retirement money that you can let grow as long as you want without being required to withdraw it.

There are options, however, that address this problem. Much like the Brandeis story, there may be a "free bridge" option for many investors.

Your financial professional will likely tell you that it is not a matter of whether or not you should perform a Roth IRA conversion, it is a matter of how much you should convert and when.

Here are some of the things to consider before converting to a Roth IRA:

- If you make a conversion before you retire, you may end up paying higher taxes on the conversion because it is likely that you are in some of your highest earning years, placing you in the highest tax bracket of your life. It is possible that a better strategy would be to wait until after you retire, a time when you may have less taxable income, which would place you in a lower tax bracket.
- Many people opt to reduce their work hours from fulltime to part-time in the years before they retire. If you have pursued this option, your income will likely be lower, in turn lowering your tax rate.
- The first years that you draw Social Security benefits can also be years of lower reported income, making it another good time frame in which to convert to a Roth IRA.

One key strategy to handling a Roth IRA conversion is to ***always be able to pay the cost of the tax conversion with outside money.***

Structuring your tax year to include something like a significant deduction can help you offset the conversion tax. This way you aren't forced to take the money you need for taxes from the value of the IRA. The reason taxes apply to this maneuver is because when you withdraw money from a traditional IRA, it is treated as taxable income by the IRS. Your financial professional, with the help of the CPAs at their firm, may be able to provide you with options like after-tax money, itemized deductions or other situations that can pose effective tax avoidance options.

Some examples of avoiding Roth IRA conversions taxes include:

- *Using medical expenses that are above 10 percent of your Adjusted Gross Income.* If you have health care costs that you can list as itemized deductions, you can convert an amount of income from a traditional IRA to a Roth IRA that is offset by the deductible amount. Essentially, deductible medical expenses negate the taxes resulting from recording the conversion.

- *Individuals, usually small business owners, who are dealing with a Net Operating Loss (NOL).* If you have NOLs, but aren't able to utilize all of them on your tax return, you can carry them forward to offset the taxable income from the taxes on income you convert to a Roth IRA.

- *Charitable giving.* If you are charitably inclined, you can use the amount of your donations to reduce the amount of taxable income you have during that year. By matching the amount you convert to a Roth IRA to the amount your taxable income was reduced by charitable giving, you can essentially avoid taxation on the conversion. You may decide to double your donations to a charity in one year, giving them two years' worth of donations in order to offset the Roth IRA conversion tax on this year's tax return.

- *Investments that are subject to depletion.* Certain investments can kick off depletion expenses. If you make an investment and are subject to depletion expenses, they can be deducted and used to offset a Roth IRA conversion tax.

Not all of the above scenarios work for everyone, and there are many other options for offsetting conversion taxes. The point is that you have options, and your financial professional and tax professional can help you understand those options.

If you have a traditional IRA, Roth conversions are something you should look at. As you approach retirement you should consider your options and make choices that keep more of your money in your pocket, not the government's.

ADDITIONAL TAX BENEFITS OF ROTH IRAS

Not only do Roth IRAs provide you with tax-advantaged growth, they also give you a tax diversified landscape that allows you to maximize your distributions. Chances are that no matter the circumstances, you will have taxed income and other assets subject to taxation. ***But if you have a Roth IRA, you have the unique ability to manage your Adjusted Gross Income (AGI), because you have a tax-advantaged income option!***

Converting to a Roth IRA can also help you preserve and build your legacy. Because Roth IRAs are exempt from RMDs, after you make a conversion from a traditional IRA, your Roth account can grow tax-advantaged for another 15, 20 or 25 years and it can be used as tax-advantaged income by your heirs. It is important to note, however, that non-spousal beneficiaries do have to take RMDs from a Roth IRA, or choose to stretch it and draw tax-advantaged income out of it over their lifetime.

TO CONVERT OR NOT TO CONVERT?

Conversions aren't only for retirees. You can convert at any time. Your choice should be based on your individual circumstances and tax situation. Sticking with a traditional IRA or converting to a Roth, again, depends on your individual circumstances, including your income, your tax bracket and the amount of deductions you have each year.

Is it better to have a Roth IRA or traditional IRA? It depends on your individual circumstance. Some people don't mind having taxable income from an IRA. Their income might not be very high and their RMD might not bump their tax bracket up, so it's not as big a deal. A similar situation might involve income from Social Security. Social Security benefits are taxed based on other income you are drawing. If you are in a position where none or very little of your Social Security benefit is subject to taxes, paying income tax on your RMD may be very easy.

> » *There are also situations where leveraging taxable income from a traditional IRA can work to your advantage come tax time. For example, Hunter and Mindy dream of buying a boat when they retire. It is something they have looked forward to their entire marriage. In addition to the savings and investments that they created to supply them with income during retirement, which includes a traditional IRA, they have also saved money for the sole purpose of purchasing a boat once they stop working.*
>
> *When the time comes and they finally buy the boat of their dreams, they pay an additional $15,000 in sales taxes that year because of the large purchase. Because they are retired and earning less money, the deductions they used to be able to realize from their income taxes are no longer there. The high amount of sales taxes they paid on the boat puts them in a*

position where they could benefit from taking taxable income from a traditional IRA.

When Hunter and Mindy's financial professional learns about their purchase, he immediately contacts a CPA at his firm to run the numbers. They determine that by taking a $15,000 distribution from their IRA, they could fulfill their income needs to offset the $15,000 sales tax deduction that they were claiming due to the purchase of their boat. In the end, they pay zero taxes on their income distribution from their IRA.

The moral of the story? **Having a tax diversified landscape gives you options.** Having capital assets that can be liquidated, tax-advantaged income options and sources that can create capital gains or capital losses will put you in a position to play your cards right no matter what you want to accomplish with your taxes. The ace up your sleeve is your financial professional and the CPAs they work with. Do yourself a favor and *plan* your taxes instead of *reporting* them!

CHAPTER 10 RECAP //

- You make more money by saving on taxes than you do by making more money. This simple concept becomes extremely valuable to people in retirement and those living on fixed incomes.
- When you report your taxes, you are paying to record history. When you *plan* your taxes with a financial professional, you are proactively finding the best options for your tax return.
- The future of U.S. taxation is uncertain. You know what the tax rate and landscape is today, but you won't tomorrow. The only thing you can really count on is the trend of increasing taxation.
- Look for the "free bridge" option in your tax strategy.
- Converting from a traditional to a Roth IRA can provide you with tax-advantaged retirement income.
- Converting to a Roth IRA can also help you preserve and build your legacy.
- There are many ways to reduce your taxes. Being smart about your Roth IRA conversion is one of the main ways to do so.

11

Going Beyond: Crafting Your Legacy

As you've seen, the importance of getting your affairs in order is essential because it secures your future and provides you with more choices. However, your future may not be the only one that you want to imbue with that safety and freedom: the futures of your loved ones may also be a crucial consideration. By getting your affairs in order, in regards to both your retirement and your estate, you ensure that your future will be protected, your final wishes are known, and your loved ones will be able to carry on with their lives with as much help as you are able to give them even after you are gone.

Additionally, the plain truth of the matter is that if you don't plan your legacy, someone else will. That someone else is usually a combination of the IRS and other government entities: lawyers, executors, courts, and accountants. Who do you think has the best interests of your beneficiaries in mind?

Today, there is more consideration given to planning a legacy than just maximizing your estate. When most people think about an estate, it may seem like something only the very wealthy have: a stately manor or an enormous business. But a legacy is something else entirely. A legacy is more than the sum total of the financial assets you have accumulated. It is the lasting impression you make on those you leave behind. The dollar and cents are just a small part of a legacy.

A legacy encompasses the stories that others tell about you, shared experiences and values. An estate may pay for college tuition, but a legacy may inform your grandchildren about the importance of higher education and self-reliance.

A legacy may also contain family heirlooms or items of emotional significance. It may be a piece of art your great-grandmother painted, family photos, or a childhood keepsake.

When you go about planning your legacy, certainly explore strategies that can maximize the financial benefit to the ones you care about. But also take the time to ensure that you have organized the whole of your legacy, and let that be a part of the last gift you leave.

Many people avoid planning their legacy until they feel they must. Something may change in your life, like the birth of a grandchild, the diagnosis of a serious health problem, or the death of a close friend or loved one. Waiting for tragedy to strike in order to get your affairs in order is not the best course of action. The emotional stress of that kind of situation can make it hard to make patient, thoughtful decisions. Taking the time to create a premeditated and thoughtful legacy plan will assure that your assets will be transferred where and when you want them when the time comes. As will be discussed below, a comprehensive legacy plan begins with making a list. The following issues should be addressed with your financial professional:

- Personal and family information
- Real estate holdings
- Investments
- Insurance
- Fiduciary appointments such as: power of attorney of financial and healthcare, guardians, executors, successor trustees
- Creating trust, will, etc.

THE BENEFITS OF PLANNING YOUR LEGACY

The distribution of your assets, whether in the form of property, stocks, Individual Retirement Accounts, 401(k)s or liquid assets, can be a complicated undertaking if you haven't left clear instructions about how you want them handled. Not having a plan will cost more money and take more time, leaving your loved ones to wait (sometimes for years) and receive less of your legacy than if you had a clear plan.

Planning your legacy will help your assets be transferred with little delay and little confusion. Instead of leaving decisions about how to distribute your estate to your family, attorneys or financial professionals, preserve your legacy and your wishes by drafting a clear plan at an early age.

And while you know all that, it can still be hard to sit down and do it. It reminds you that life is short, and the relatively complicated nature of sorting through your assets can feel like a daunting task. But one thing is for sure: *it is impossible for your assets to be transferred or distributed the way you want at the end of your life if you don't have a plan.*

Ask yourself:

- Are my assets up to date?

- Have my primary and contingent beneficiaries been clearly designated?
- Does my plan allow for restriction of a beneficiary?
- Does my legacy plan address minor children that I want to provide with income?
- Does my legacy plan allow for multi-generational payout? Answers to these questions are critical if you want the final say in how your assets are distributed. In order to achieve your legacy goals, you need a plan.

MAKING A PLAN

Eventually, when your income need is filled and you have sufficient standby money to meet your need for emergencies, travel or other extra expenses you are planning for, whatever isn't used during your lifetime becomes your financial legacy. The money that you do not use during your lifetime will either go to loved ones, unloved ones, charity, or the IRS. The question is, who would you rather disinherit?

By having a legacy plan that clearly outlines your assets, your beneficiaries and your distribution goals, you can make sure that your money and property is ending up in the hands of the people you determine beforehand. Is it really that big of a deal? It absolutely is. Think about it. Without a clear plan, it is impossible for anyone to know if your beneficiary designations are current and reflect your wishes because you haven't clearly expressed who your beneficiaries are. You may have an idea of who you want your assets to go to, but without a plan, it is anyone's guess. It is also impossible to know if the titling of your assets is accurate unless you have gone through and determined whose name is on the titles. More importantly, *if you have not clearly and effectively communicated your desires regarding the planned distribution of your legacy, you and your family may end up losing a large part of it.*

As you can see, managing a legacy is more complicated than having an attorney read your will, divide your estate and write checks to your heirs. The additional issue of taxes, Family Maximum Benefit calculations and a host of other decisions rear their heads. Educating yourself about the best options for positioning your legacy assets is a challenging undertaking. Working with a financial professional who is versed in determining the most efficient and effective ways of preserving and distributing your legacy can save you time, money and strife.

So, how do you begin?

Making a Legacy Plan Starts with a Simple List. The first, and one of the largest, steps to setting up an estate plan with a financial professional that reflects your desires is creating a detailed inventory of your assets and debts (if you have any). You need to know what assets you have, who the beneficiaries are, how much they are worth and how they are titled. You can start by identifying and listing your assets. This is a good starting point for working with a financial professional who can then help you determine the detailed information about your assets that will dictate how they are distributed upon your death. Moreover, this would also be a good time to assign power of attorney to someone.

If you are particularly concerned about leaving your kids and grandkids a lifetime of income with minimal taxes, you will want to discuss a Stretch IRA option with your financial professional.

STRETCH IRAS: GETTING THE MOST OUT OF YOUR MONEY

In 1986, the U.S. Congress passed a law that allows for multi-generational distributions of IRA assets. This type of distribution is called a Stretch IRA because it stretches the distribution of the account out over a longer period of time to several beneficiaries. It also allows the account to continue accumulating value throughout your relatives' lifetimes. You can use a Stretch IRA as an income tool that distributes throughout your lifetime, your children's lifetimes and your grandchildren's lifetimes.

Stretch IRAs are an attractive option for those more concerned with creating income for their loved ones than leaving them with a lump sum that may be subject to a high tax rate. With traditional IRA distributions, non-spousal beneficiaries must generally take distributions from their inherited IRAs, whether transferred or not, within five years after the death of the IRA owner. An exception to this rule applies if the beneficiary elects to take distributions over his or her lifetime, which is referred to as stretching the IRA.

Let's begin by looking at the potential of stretching an IRA throughout multiple generations.

> » *Solomon has an IRA with a current balance of $350,000. If we assume a five percent annual rate of return, and a 28 percent tax rate, the Stretch IRA turned a $502,625 legacy into more than $1.5 million. Doubling the value of the IRA also provided Solomon, his wife, two children and three grandchildren with income. Not choosing the stretch option would have cost nearly $800,000 and had impacts on six of Solomon's loved ones.*

Unfortunately, many things may also play a role in failing to stretch IRA distributions. It can be tempting for a beneficiary to take a lump sum of money despite the tax consequences. Fortunately, if you want to solidify your plan for distribution, there are options that will allow you to open up an IRA and incorporate "spendthrift" clauses for your beneficiaries. This will ensure your legacy is stretched appropriately and to your specifications. Only certain insurance companies allow this option, and you will not find this benefit with any brokerage accounts. You need to work with a financial professional who has the appropriate relationship with an insurance company that provides this option.

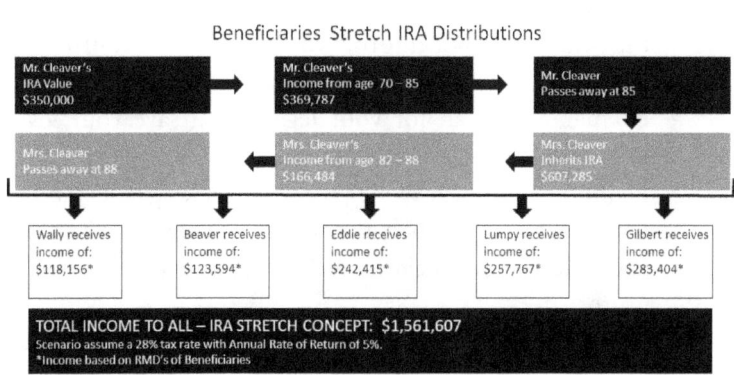

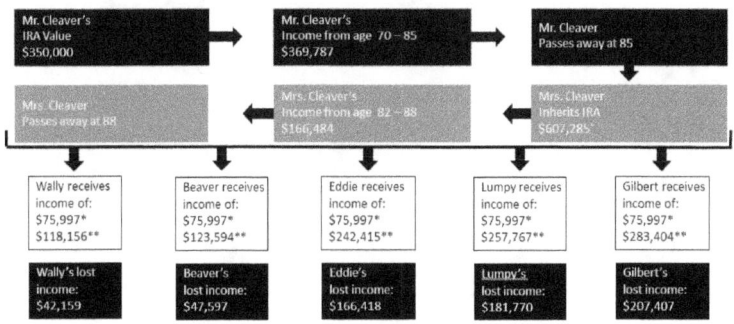

CHAPTER 11 RECAP //

- If you want your wishes to be followed, you need to make them known.
- If you don't plan your legacy, someone else will and because this will be the last imprint you will leave of yourself, it's important to make sure it's the one you want.
- By making a plan for your legacy, you save your loved ones undue stress, time and money.
- Planning your legacy begins with making a list of all your assets, how much they're worth, how they're titled and who the beneficiaries are. Make sure this list is kept up-to-date.
- Stretch IRAs can be a great way to stretch the distribution of your retirement account over a longer period of time to several beneficiaries.

12

An End of the Affair:
Final Estate Preparations

Terry organized his assets long ago. He started planning his retirement early and made investment decisions that would meet his needs. With a combination of IRA to Roth IRA conversions, a series of income annuities and a well-planned money management strategy overseen by his financial professional, he easily filled his income gap and was able to focus on ways to accumulate his wealth throughout his retirement. He reorganized his Know So and Hope So Money as he got older. When Terry retired, he had an income plan created that allowed him to maximize his Social Security benefit. He even had enough to accumulate wealth during his retirement. At this point, Terry turned his attention to planning his legacy. He wanted to know how he could maximize the amount of his legacy he will pass on to his heirs.

Terry met with an attorney to draw up a will, but he quickly learned that while having a will was a good plan, it wasn't the most efficient way to distribute his legacy. In fact, relying solely on a will created several roadblocks.

The two main problems that arose for Terry were *Probate* and *Unintentional Disinheritance:*

Problem #1: Probate

Probate. Just speaking the word out loud can cause shivers to run down your spine. Probate's ugly reputation is well deserved. It can be a costly, time consuming process that diminishes your estate and can delay the distribution of your estate to your loved ones. Nasty stuff, by any measure. Unless you have made a clear legacy plan and discussed options for avoiding probate, it is highly likely that you have many assets that might pass through probate needlessly. ***If your will and beneficiary designations aren't correctly structured, some of these assets will go through the probate process, which can turn dollars into cents.***

Even the basic purpose of probate is rather harsh and unforgiving: it is to determine who gets what from the dead. Many people think that if they have a will, then their assets will be able to circumvent the probate process. Unfortunately, this is just a misnomer and a rather dangerous and costly one at that. While there are cases when the presence of a will basically reduces probate to being just a formality so there is not much risk that your will won't be executed per your instructions, this is not something that you should count on: the final beneficiary decisions will be decided by the probate judge, not necessarily by the wishes expressed in your will. By its very nature, probate is extremely mercurial, expensive, lengthy and ponderous.

A typical probate process identifies all of your assets and debts, pays any taxes and fees that you owe (including estate tax), pays court fees, and distributes your property and assets to your heirs. This process usually takes at least a year, and can take even longer before your heirs actually receive anything that you have left for them. For this reason, and because of the sometimes exorbitant fees that may be charged by lawyers and accountants during the process, probate has earned a nasty reputation. To add insult to injury, probate can also be a painstakingly public process. Because the probate process happens in court, the assets you own that go through a probate procedure become part of the public record. While this may not seem like a big deal to some, other people don't want that kind of intimate information available to the public.

Additionally, if your estate is entirely distributed via your will, the money that your family may need to cover the costs of your medical bills, funeral expenses and estate taxes will be tied up in probate, which can last up to a year or more. While immediate family members may have the option of requesting immediate cash from your assets during probate to cover immediate health care expenses, taxes, and fees, that process comes with its own set of complications. Choosing alternative methods for distributing your legacy can make life easier for your loved ones and can help them claim more of your estate in a more timely fashion than traditional methods.

A simpler and less tedious approach is to avoid probate altogether by structuring your estate to be distributed outside of the probate process. There are several common methods you can employ to accomplish this: one is to structure your assets inside a life insurance plan, another is to use individual retirement planning tools like IRAs that give you the option of designating a beneficiary upon your death, and, another option would be to transfer all your assets into a revocable trust.

Problem #2: Unintentionally Disinheriting Your Family

You would never want to unintentionally disinherit a loved one or loved ones because of confusion surrounding your legacy plan. Unfortunately, it happens. Why? This terrible situation is typically caused by a simple lack of understanding. In particular, mistakes regarding legacy distribution occur with regards to those whom people care for the most: their grandchildren.

One of the most important ways to plan for the inheritance of your grandchildren is by properly structuring the distribution of your legacy. Specifically, you need to know if your legacy is going to be distributed *per stirpes* or *per capita*.

Per Stirpes. *Per stirpes* is a legal term in Latin that means "by the branch." Your estate will be distributed *per stirpes* if you designate each branch of your family to receive an equal share of your estate. In the event that your children predecease you, their share will be distributed evenly between their children — your grandchildren.

Per Capita. *Per capita* distribution is different in that you may designate different amounts of your estate to be distributed to members of the same generation.

Per stirpes distribution of assets will follow the family tree down the line as the predecessor beneficiaries pass away. On the other hand, per capita distribution of assets ends on the branch of the family tree with the death of a designated beneficiary. For example, when your child passes away, in a per capita distribution, your grandchildren would not receive distributions from the assets that you designated to your child.

What the terms mean is not nearly as important as what they do, however. The reality is that improperly titled assets could accidentally leave your grandchildren disinherited upon the death of their parents. It's easy to check, and it's even easier to fix.

A simple way to remember the difference between the two types of distribution goes something like this: "*Stripes are forever and Capita is capped.*"

Of course, the best way to avoid this problem is to simply go over all your assets with your financial planner and make sure they are properly titled and up to date. No legacy plan is complete until you have carefully examined the asset distribution and double-checked that all your beneficiaries and heirs are properly accommodated and accounted for.

TRUST VERSUS WILLS

If you want to avoid the expense, publicity, stress, duration, and equivocal nature of probate then it's crucial you have a conversation with an elder law attorney and your financial professional about whether establishing a living trust would be a fortuitous strategy to utilize. A living or revocable trust is a document that allows you to transfer all of your assets to a trust so that none of your assets are titled in your name, which means it is no longer in your estate and your assets will simply be held in the trust (unless you decide to transfer them out by having them retitled). You will also select a beneficiary or trustee for the trust. When you die, all of your assets will be owned by the trust instead of by you, which means your assets will bypass the probate process and the trustee you chose would be given control of the trust and, thus, all your assets.

In addition to the very appealing notion of avoiding probate, there are several other significant differences between a living or revocable trust and a will. For example, a will, because it endures the probate process, can be challenged. Consequently, anyone can challenge any provision in your will, which can further delay the process, increase the expense, and distort your final wishes. A trust, on the other hand, cannot be challenged so your wishes will be followed. Moreover, having a trust will ensure your affairs are privately and quickly settled. Another advantage of establishing a revocable trust is that it is a legal document that is reciprocal in all states, whereas a will is not. In other words, if you made a will in Ohio but also had property in Montana, then that property would have to go through the probate process in Montana. The provisions of a trust will not be undone by moving between states.

The benefits to establishing a living trust are well worth investigating. As you continue to move forward with the steps necessary to get your affairs in order, entertain the idea that a living trust may be an efficient way to preserve your assets from being whittled away by fees and the like and more effectively secure your loved ones' futures. Granted, establishing a trust is more expensive than drawing up a will. While most wills cost next to nothing to write, setting up a trust costs about $2,000 on average but can range anywhere between $700 and $5,000. However, bear in mind that even though a trust is more expensive up front, there will generally be no other fees to contend with once the trust has been established.

LIFE INSURANCE: AN IMPORTANT LEGACY TOOL

As discussed earlier, a good life insurance policy can prove to be one of the most effective and versatile financial vehicles with which you ever engage. All though some of these points have already been mentioned, let's go over the concept and mechanics of a life insurance in regards to legacy planning and organizing your estate. Life insurance is a highly efficient legacy tool because it creates money when it is needed or desired the most. Over the years, life insurance has become less expensive, while it offers more features, and it provides longer guarantees.

There are many unique benefits of life insurance that can help your beneficiaries get the most out of your legacy. Some of them include:

- Providing beneficiaries with a tax-free, liquid asset.

- Covering the costs associated with your death.
- Providing income for your dependents.
- Offering an investment opportunity for your beneficiaries.
- Covering expenses such as tuition or mortgage down payments for your children or grandchildren.

Very few people want life insurance, but nearly everyone wants what it does. Life insurance is specifically, and uniquely, capable of creating money when it is needed most. When a loved one passes, no amount of money can remove the pain of loss. And certainly, money doesn't solve the challenges that might arise with losing someone important.

It has been said that when you have money, you have options. When you don't have money, your options are severely limited. You might imagine a life insurance policy can give your family and loved ones options that would otherwise be impossible.

> » Ben spent the last 20 years building a small business. In so many ways, it is a family business. Each of his three children, Maddie, Ruby and Edward, worked in the shop part-time during high school. But after all three attended college, only Maddie returned to join her father, and eventually will run the business full-time when Ben retires.
>
> Ben is able to retire comfortably on Social Security and on-going income from the shop, but the business is nearly his entire financial legacy. It is his wish that Maddie own the business outright, but he also wants to leave an equal legacy to each of his three children.
>
> There is no simple way to divide the business into thirds and still leave the business intact for Maddie.
>
> Ben ends up buying a life insurance policy to make up the difference. Ruby and Edward will receive their share of an

inheritance in cash from the life insurance policy and Maddie will be able to inherit the business intact.

Ben is able to accomplish his goals, treat all three children equitably and leave Maddie the business she helped to build.

If you have a life insurance policy but you haven't looked at it in a while, you may not know how it operates, how much it is worth and how it will be distributed to your beneficiaries. You may also need to update your beneficiaries on your policy. In short, without a comprehensive review of your policy, you don't really know where the money will go or to whom it will go.

If you don't have a life insurance policy but are looking for options to maintain and grow your legacy, speaking with a professional can show you the benefits of life insurance. Many people don't consider buying a life insurance policy until some event in their life triggers it, like the loss of a loved one, an accident or a health condition.

BENEFITS OF LIFE INSURANCE

Life insurance is a useful and secure tool for contingency planning, ensuring that your dependents receive the assets that you want them to have, and for meeting the financial goals you have set for the future. As discussed previously, while it bears the name "Life Insurance," it is, in reality, a diverse financial tool that can meet many needs. The main function of a life insurance policy is to provide financial assets for your survivors. Life insurance is particularly efficient at achieving this goal because it provides a tax-advantaged lump sum of money in the form of a death benefit to your beneficiary or beneficiaries. That financial asset can be used in a number of ways. It can be structured as an investment to provide income for your spouse or children, it can pay down debts, and it can be used to cover estate taxes and other costs associated with death.

Tax liabilities on the estate you leave behind are inevitable. Capital property, for instance, is taxed at its fair market value at the time of your death, unless that property is transferred to your spouse. If the property has appreciated during the time you owned it, taxation on capital gains will occur. Registered Retirement Savings Plans (RRSPs) and other similarly structured assets are also included as taxable income unless transferred to a beneficiary as well. Those are just a few examples of how an estate can become subject to a heavy tax burden. The unique benefits of a life insurance policy provide ways to handle this tax burden, solving any liquidity problems that may arise if your family members want to hold onto an illiquid asset, such as a piece of property or an investment. Life insurance can provide a significant amount of money to a family member or other beneficiary, and that money is likely to remain exempt from taxation or seizure.

One of life insurance's most important benefits is that it is not considered part of the estate of the policy holder. The death benefit that is paid by the insurance company goes exclusively to the beneficiaries listed on the policy. This shields the proceeds of the policy from fees and costs that can reduce an estate, including probate proceedings, attorneys' fees and claims made by creditors. The distribution of your life insurance policy is also unaffected by delays of the estate's distribution, like probate. Your beneficiaries will get the proceeds of the policy in a timely fashion, regardless of how long it takes for the rest of your estate to be settled.

Investing a portion of your assets in a life insurance policy can also protect that portion of your estate from creditors. If you owe money to someone or some entity at the time of your death, a creditor is not able to claim any money from a life insurance policy or an annuity, for that matter. As an exception to this rule, if you had already used the life insurance policy as collateral against a loan. If a large portion of the money you want to dedicate to your legacy is sitting in a savings account, investment or other liquid form, creditors may be able to receive their claim on it before your beneficiaries get anything,that is if there's anything left. A life insurance policy protects your assets from creditors and ensures that your beneficiaries get the money that you intend them to have.

HOW MUCH LIFE INSURANCE DO YOU NEED?

Determining the type of policy and the amount right for you depends on an analysis of your needs. A financial professional can help you complete a needs analysis that will highlight the amount of insurance that you require to meet your goals. This type of personalized review will allow you to determine ways to continue providing income for your spouse or any dependents you may have. A financial professional can also help you calculate the amount of income that your policy should replace to meet the needs of your beneficiaries and the duration of the distribution of that income.

You may also want to use your life insurance policy to meet any expenses associated with your death. These can include funeral costs, fees from probate and legal proceedings, and taxes. You may also want to dedicate a portion of your policy proceeds to help fund tuition or other expenses for your children or grandchildren. You can buy a policy and hope it covers all of those costs, or you can work with a professional who can calculate exactly how much insurance you need and how to structure it to meet your goals. Which would you rather do?

AVOIDING POTENTIAL SNAGS

There are benefits to having life insurance supersede the direction given in a will or other estate plan, but there are also some potential snags that you should address to meet your wishes. For example, if your will instructs that your assets be divided equally between your two children but your life insurance beneficiary is listed as just one of the children, the assets in the life insurance policy will only be distributed to the child listed as the beneficiary. The beneficiary designation of your life insurance supersedes your will or living trust's instruction. This is important to understand when designating beneficiaries on a policy you purchase. Work with a professional to make sure that your beneficiaries are accurately listed on your assets, especially your life insurance policies.

USING LIFE INSURANCE TO BUILD YOUR LEGACY

Depending on your goals, there are strategies you can use that could multiply how much you leave behind. Life insurance is one of the most surefire and efficient investment tools for building a substantial legacy that will meet your financial goals.

Here is a brief overview of how life insurance can boost your legacy:

- Life insurance provides an immediate increase in your legacy.
- It provides an income tax-advantaged death benefit for your beneficiaries.
- A good life insurance policy has the opportunity to accumulate value over time.
- It may have an option to include long-term care (LTC) or chronic illness benefits should you require them.

If your Green Money income needs for retirement are met and you have Yellow Money assets that will provide for your future expenses, you may have extra assets that you want to earmark as legacy funds. By electing to invest those assets into a life insurance policy, you can immediately increase the amount of your legacy. Remember, **life insurance allows you to transfer a tax-advantaged lump sum of money to your beneficiaries. It remains in your control during your lifetime, can provide for your long-term care needs and bypasses probate costs.** And make no mistake, taxes can have a huge impact on your legacy.

Not only that, income and assets from your legacy can have tax implications for your beneficiaries, as well.

Here's a brief overview of how taxes could affect your legacy and your beneficiaries:

- The higher your income, the higher the rate at which it is taxed.
- Withdrawals from qualified plans are taxed as income.
- What's more, when you leave a large qualified plan, it ends up being taxed at a high rate.
- If you left a $500,000 IRA to your child, they could end up owing as much as $140,000 in income taxes.
- However, if you could just withdraw $50,000 a year, the tax bill might only be $10,000 per year.

How could you use that annual amount to leave a larger legacy? Luckily, you can leverage a life insurance policy to avoid those tax penalties, preserving a larger amount of your legacy and freeing your beneficiaries from an added tax burden.

> » *When Cammie turned 70 years old, she decided it was time to look into life insurance policy options. She still feels young, but she remembers that her mother died in early 70s, and she wants to plan ahead so she can pass on some of her legacy to her grandchildren just like her grandmother did for her.*
>
> *Cammie doesn't really want to think about life insurance, but she does want the security, reliability and tax-advantaged distribution that it offers. She lives modestly, and her Social Security benefit meets most of her income needs. As the beneficiary of her late husband's Certificate of Deposit (CD), she has $100,000 in an account that she has never used and doesn't anticipate ever needing since her income needs were already met.*

*After looking at several different investment options with a professional, Cammie decides that a Single Premium life insurance policy fits her needs best. She can buy the policy with a $100,000 one-time payment and she is guaranteed that it would provide more than the value of the contract to her beneficiaries. If she left the money in the CD, it would be subject to taxes. But for every dollar that she puts into the life insurance policy, her beneficiaries are guaranteed at least that dollar plus a death benefit, and all of it will be **tax-free!***

For $100,000, Cammie's particular policy offers a $170,000 death benefit distribution to her beneficiaries. By moving the $100,000 from a CD to a life insurance policy, Cammie increases her legacy by 70 percent. Not only that, she has also sheltered it from taxes, so her beneficiaries will be able to receive $1.70 for every $1.00 that she entered into the policy! While buying the policy doesn't allow her to use the money for herself, it does allow her family to benefit from her well-planned legacy.

MAKE YOUR WISHES KNOWN

Estate taxes used to be a much hotter topic in the mid-2000s when the estate tax limits and exclusions were much smaller and taxed at a higher rate than today. In 2008, estates valued at $2 million or more were taxed at 45 percent. Just two years later, the limit was raised to $5 million dollars taxed at 35 percent. The limit has continued to rise ever since. The limit applies to fewer people than before. Estate organization, however, is just as important as ever, and it affects everyone.

Ask yourself:

- Are your assets actually titled and held the way you think they are?
- Are your beneficiaries set up the way you think they should be?

- Have there been changes to your family or those you desire as beneficiaries?

There is more to your legacy beyond your property, money, investments and other assets that you leave to family members, loved ones and charities. Everyone has a legacy beyond money. You also leave behind personal items of importance, your values and beliefs, your personal and family history, and your wishes. Beyond a will and a plan for your assets, it is important that you make your wishes known to someone for the rest of your personal legacy. When it comes time for your family and loved ones to make decisions after you are gone, knowing your wishes can help them make decisions that honor you and your legacy, and give meaning to what you leave behind.

Think about your:
- Personal stories / recollections / Values
- Personal items of emotional significance
- Financial assets
- Do you want to make a plan to pass these things on to your family?

Failure to properly plan your legacy can have profound repercussions: not only will your family receive a fraction of the assets they might otherwise have been entitled to, but also your estate will become open to the public. To save your family money and protect yourself from scrutiny, don't make the same mistake as the people listed below and take the time now to develop a thorough plan for your estate:

CELEBRITY ESTATE	GROSS ESTATE	SETTLEMENT COST	NET ESTATE	TOTAL LOSS
FRANKLIN D. ROOSEVELT	$1,940,999	$329,739	$554,887	37%
HUMPHREY BOGART	$910,146	$274,234	$635,912	30%
WILLIAM E. BOEING	$22,386,158	$10,589,748	$11,796,410	47%
WALT DISNEY	$23,004,851	$6,811,943	$16,192,908	30%
MARILYN MONROE	$819,176	$448,750	$370,426	55%
ELVIS PRESLEY	$10,165,434	$7,374,635	$2,790,799	73%
J.P. MORGAN	$17,121,482	$11,893,691	$5,227,791	69%
JOHN D. ROCKEFELLER	$26,905,182	$17,124,988	$9,780,194	64%
FREDERICK VANDERBILT	$76,838,530	$42,846,112	$33,992,418	56%

Once you have made a legacy plan, remember that it can still be adjusted. In fact, it should be. To make sure that your plan still accurately reflects your wishes, review it every few years or after a major life event such as:

- Divorce
- Death
- Marriage
- Change in employment
- Inheritance
- Other significant financial change
- Relocation to another state
- Sale or purchase of real estate
- Change in physical or mental ability of anyone named in your estate-planning documents
- Major estate-planning law or tax law changes

WORKING WITH A PROFESSIONAL

Part of using life insurance to your greatest advantage is selecting the policy and provider that can best meet your goals. Venturing into the jungle of policies, brokers and salespeople can be overwhelming, and can leave you wondering if you've made the best decision. Working with a trusted financial professional can help you cut through the red tape, the "sales-speak" and confusion to find a policy that meets your goals and best serves your desires for your money. If you already have a policy, a financial professional can help you review it and become familiar with the policy's premium, the guarantees the policy affords, its performance, and its features and benefits. A financial professional can also help you make any necessary changes to the policy.

> » *When Cheryl turned 88, her daughter finally convinced her to meet with a financial professional to help her organize her assets and get her legacy in order. Although Cheryl is reluctant to let a stranger in on her personal finances, she ends up very glad that she did.*
>
> *In the process of listing Cheryl's assets and her beneficiaries, her professional finds a man's name listed as the beneficiary of an old life insurance annuity that she owns. It turns out, the man is Cheryl's ex-husband who is still alive. Had Cheryl passed away before her ex-husband, the annuities and any death benefits that came with them, would have been passed on to her ex-husband. This does not reflect her latest wishes.*

Things change, relationships evolve and the way you would like your legacy organized needs to adapt to the changes that happen throughout your life. There may be a new child or grandchild in your family, or you may have been divorced or remarried. A professional will regularly review your legacy assets and ask you questions to make sure that everything is up to date and that the current organization reflects your current wishes. Furthermore, make sure that every time you update your legacy plan, you dispose of the old one! A lot of unnecessary confusion can be caused when old wills are found after a loved one passes but the heirs don't know they are not referencing the most current version.

As you've seen, getting your affairs in order is no small task. It involves shifting from an earning and saving financial paradigm to an asset leveraging one so that you can develop a retirement plan that positions your assets in a way that allows them to sustainably generate a lifetime supply of income for you. Moreover, it requires having a strategy in place that will meet your end-of-life long-term health care needs without risking your assets and, finally, it necessitates creating a will or trust that clearly dictates the way you would like your assets to be distributed to your loved ones. Additionally, all of these goals need to be accomplished in the most expeditious, least expensive and tax avoidant way possible. In other words, getting your affairs in order is a huge undertaking that requires restructuring your assets to accomplish two main objectives. The first goal is that your assets should be able to provide you with retirement income but still be quite well insulated from market volatility and other external influences, while the second goal decrees that your assets will be protected from taxes and other estate costs after you die so that your assets will be preserved and expeditiously passed on to your beneficiaries.

This is by no means an impossible task, but it does require careful deliberation and the help of several financial professionals. For example, getting your affairs in order would most likely require, at least, a Registered Investment Advisor, a CPA, an elder-law attorney and an estate planner. While all of these individuals would be there to serve a specific and vital purpose, they would also all be telling you what to do but none of them would be telling you what they're doing for you. Put another way: there would be too many cooks in the kitchen! You need a head chef to direct, oversee and coordinate all the activity. When it comes to getting your affairs in order, you need a central person who would have a clear view and understanding of the big picture and be able to make decisions and arrangements accordingly.

It can be useful to think of it using the following analogy: at this point in your life, you most likely see a variety of different specialist doctors who are all working to ameliorate your health issues, but each does so through the scope of his particular specialty. While the contribution of each specialist is meaningful, their efficacy would be greatly diminished if your general practitioner was not overseeing and coordinating all their different diagnoses and courses of treatments. An estate planner is like the general practitioner of your finances. In other words, you need an estate planner to act as a traffic cop for your plan.

An "estate planner" will be able to make sure that the legal, financial, and familial components of your estate plan are well organized, communicating with each other and working in concert to most effectively execute your wishes. Getting your affairs in order can be incredibly challenging but it is also incredibly rewarding. You have spent your life working hard for your money and this is the time to make sure you implement the necessary provisions so it will be there when you need it during retirement and there for your loved ones when you pass.

CHAPTER 12 RECAP //

- You can structure your assets in ways that maximize distributions to your beneficiaries.

- Working with a financial professional can help ensure that many of your assets avoid the ponderous and expensive probate process.

- A financial professional can help review the details of the assets you have designated to be a part of your legacy and make sure that you aren't unintentionally disinheriting your heirs.

- Life insurance provides the distribution of tax-free, liquid assets to your beneficiaries.

- Investing in a life insurance policy can significantly build your legacy.

- Organizing your estate will allow you to make sure your wishes are properly carried through.

- You can take advantage of a "Stretch IRA" to provide income for you, your spouse and your beneficiaries throughout their lifetimes.

- Understand if your assets will be distributed *per stirpes* or *per capita*.

- Working with a financial professional can help you select the policy that best meets your needs, or can help you fine tune your existing policy to better reflect your desires and intentions.

13

Choosing a Financial Professional

From the moment you dip your toes into the retirement planning pool to the point you start swimming laps, your assets organized, your income needs met, and your accumulation and legacy plans in place, working with a professional that you trust can make all the difference in how well your retirement reflects your desires.

It is important to know what you are looking for before taking the plunge. There are many people that would love to handle your money, but not everyone is qualified to handle it in a way that leads to a holistic approach to creating a solid retirement plan.

The distinction being made here is that you should look for someone that puts your interests first and actively wants to help you meet your goals and objectives. Oftentimes, the products someone sells you matter less than their dedication to making sure that you have a plan that meets your needs.

Professionals take your whole financial position into consideration. They make plans that adjust your risk exposure, invest in tools that secure your desired income during retirement and create investment strategies that allow you to continue accumulating wealth during your retirement for you to use later or to contribute to your legacy. If you buy stocks with a broker, use a different agent for a life insurance policy and have an unmanaged 401(k) through your employer, working with a financial professional and an estate planner will consolidate the management of your assets so you have one trustworthy person quarterbacking all of the team elements of your portfolio. Financial products and investment tools change, but the concepts that lie behind wise retirement planning are lasting. In the end, a financial professional's approach is designed for those serious about getting their affairs in order. *Can you say the same thing about the person that advises you about your financial life?*

Recall the analogy used in the last chapter that compared an estate planner to a general health practitioner. While this analogy is useful to explain the coordination role an estate planner takes on, let's apply this analogy in a slightly different way to illustrate the importance of selecting the right financial professional: there are many different specialties and branches of medicine that exist. If your left eye saw black spots for several days, you would probably go see an ophthalmologist and not a cardiologist, because you would want a doctor who specialized in your problem area. Likewise, there are different branches of finance. If you just turned 30 years old and have your whole life ahead of you to invest, you'd probably choose a financial professional who specializes in wealth accumulation products that are higher risk because they would be the most familiar with those tools and strategies. However, if you were nearing the end of your life you would probably want a financial professional who works with more seniors so he or she will be familiar with the needs of your situation. It all depends on your particular circumstance, preference, and how comfortable you are with him or her.

When it comes to estate planning, you can either choose an accredited estate planner or you can choose a financial professional who has significant estate organization experience. The key is to make sure that one person has both the capacity and the information needed to coordinate the implementation of your plan.

It's easy to see how choosing a financial professional can be one of the most important decisions you can make in your life. Not only do they provide you with advice, they also manage the personal assets that supply your retirement income and contribute to your legacy. So, how do you find a good one?

HOW TO FIND A FINANCIAL PROFESSIONAL YOU CAN TRUST

Taking care to select a financial professional is one of the best things you can do for yourself and for your future. Your professional has influence and control of your investment decisions, making their role in your life more than just important. Your financial security and the quality of your retirement depends on the decisions, investment strategies and asset structuring that you and your professional create.

Working with a professional is different than calling up a broker when you want to buy or trade some stock. This isn't a decision that you can hand off to anyone else. You need to bring your time and attention to the table when it comes to finding someone with whom you can entrust your financial life. Separating the wheat from the chaff will take some work, but you'll be happy you did it.

While no one can tell you exactly who to choose or how to choose them, the following information can help you narrow the field:

- You can start by asking your friends, family and colleagues for referrals. You will want to pay particular attention to the recommendations that you get from others who are in your similar financial situation and who have similar lifestyle choices. The professional for the CEO of your company may have a different skill-set than the skill-set of the professional befitting your cousin who has 3 kids and a Subaru like you. Do follow-up research on the Internet as well. Look up the people who have been recommended to you on websites like LinkedIn that show the work history, referrals and experience of the candidates that you find most attractive. You will also learn about the firms with or for whom they work. The investment philosophies and reputations of the companies they work for will tell you a lot about how they will handle your money.

- The other side of the coin, however, is that everyone and their brother has a recommendation about how you should manage your money and who should manage it for you. From hot stock tips to "the best money manager in the state," people love to share good information that makes them look like they are in-the-know. Nobody wants to talk about the bad stock purchases they made, the times they lost money and the poor selections they made regarding financial professionals or stock brokers. If you decide to take a friend or family member's recommendation, make sure they have a substantial, long-term experience with the financial professional and that their glowing review isn't just based on a one-time "win."

- You can also use online tools like the search function of the Financial Planning Association (http://www.fpanet. org/) and the National Association of Personal Financial Advisors (http://www.napfa.org/). Most of the profession-als listed on these sites do not earn commissions from selling financial products, but are instead paid on a fee-only basis for their services. It is important to understand how your professional is being paid. It is generally considered preferable to work with a fee-based professional who will not have conflicts of interests between earning a commission and acting in your best interests.

- Many professionals may also be brokers or dealers that can earn commissions on things like life insurance, certain types of annuities and disability insurance. These professionals have most likely intentionally overlapped their roles so that if their clients choose to purchase insurance or investment products that require a broker or dealer, those clients won't have to find an additional person to work with. Again, understanding the role of your professional will help you make your determination.

NARROWING THE FIELD

1. Decide on the Type of Professional with Whom You Want to Work. There are four basic kinds of financial professionals. Many professionals may play overlapping roles. It is important to know a professional's primary function, how they charge for their services and whether they are obligated to act in your best interest.

Registered representatives, better known as stockbrokers or bank / investment representatives, make their living by earning commissions on insurance products and investment services. Stockbrokers basically sell you things. The products from which they make the highest commission are sometimes the products that they recommend to their clients. If you want to make a simple transaction, such as buying or selling a particular stock, a registered representative can help you. Although registered representatives are licensed professionals, if you want to create a structured and planful approach to positioning your assets for retirement, you might want to consider continuing your search.

The term "planner" is often misused. It can refer to credible professionals that are CPAs, CFPs and ChFCs to your uncle's next door neighbor who claims to have a lead on some undervalued stock about to be "discovered." A wide array of people may claim to be planners because there are no requirements to be a planner. The term financial planner, however, refers to someone who is properly registered as an investment advisor and serves as a fiduciary as described below.

Financial professionals are the diamonds in the rough. These Registered Investment Advisors are compensated on a fee basis. They do, however, often have licensure as stockbrokers or insurance agents, allowing them to earn commissions on certain transactions. More importantly, **financial professionals are financial fiduciaries, meaning they are required to make financial decisions in your best interest and reflecting your risk tolerance.** Investment Advisors are held to high ethical standards and are highly regarded in the financial industry. Financial professionals also often take a more comprehensive approach to asset management. These professionals are trained and credentialed to plan and coordinate their clients' assets in order to meet their goals or retirement and legacy planning. They are not focused on individual stocks, investments or markets. They look at the big picture, the whole enchilada.

Money managers are on par with financial professionals. However, they are often given explicit permission to make investment decisions without advanced approval by their clients.

Understanding who you are working with and what their title is the first step to planning your retirement. While each of the above-mentioned types of financial professionals can help you with aspects of your finances, it is **financial professionals** who have the most intimate role, the most objective investment strategies and the most unbiased mode of compensation for their services. A financial professional can also help you with the nonfinancial aspects of your legacy and can help you find ways to create a tax planning strategy to help you save money.

2. Be Objective. At the end of the day, you need to separate the weak from the strong. While you might want a strong personal rapport with your professional, or you may want to choose your professional for their personality and positive attitude, it is more important that you find someone who will give sage advice regarding achieving your retirement goals.

It can be helpful to use a process of elimination to narrow the field of potential professionals. Look into five or six potential leads and cross off your list the ones that don't meet your requirements until only one or two remain. Cross-check your remaining choices against the list of things you need from a professional. Make sure they represent a firm that has the investment tools and products that you desire, and make sure they have experience in retirement planning. That is, after all, the main goal.

Don't be afraid to investigate each of your candidates. You'll want to ask the same questions and look for the same information from everyone you consider so you can then compare them and discern which is best for you. You'll want to take a look at the specific credentials of each professional, their experience and competence, their ethics and fiduciary status, their history and track record, and a list of the services that they offer. The professionals who meet all or most of your qualifications are the ones you will contact for an interview.

Potential professionals should meet your qualifications in the following categories:

- *Credentials:* Look at their experience, the quality of their education, any associations to which they belong and certifications they have earned. Someone who has continued their professional education through ongoing certifications will be more up-to-date on current financial practices compared to someone who got their degree 25 years ago and hasn't done a thing since.

- *Practices:* Look at the track record of your candidates, how they are compensated for their services, the reports and analysis they offer, and their value added services.
- *Services:* Your professional must meet your needs. If you are planning your retirement, you should work with someone who offers services that help you to that end. You want someone who can offer planning, advice on investment strategies, ways to calculate risk, advice on insurance and annuities products, and ways to manage your tax strategy.
- *Ethics:* You want to work with someone who is above board and does things the right way. Vet them by checking their compliance record, current licensing, fiduciary status and, yes, even their criminal record. You never know!

3. Ask for and Check References. Once you have selected two or three professionals that you want to meet, call or email them and ask for references. Every professional should be able to provide you with at least two or three names. In fact, they will probably be eager to share them with you. Most professionals rely on references for validation of their success, quality of services and likability. You should, however, take them with a grain of salt. You have no way to know whether or not references are a professional's friends or colleagues.

It is worth contacting references, however, to check for inconsistencies. Ask each reference the same set of questions to get the same basic information. How long have they been working with the professional? What kind of services have they used and were they happy with them? What type of financial planning did they use the professional for? Were they versed in the type of financial planning that you needed? You can also ask them direct questions to elicit candid responses. What was the full cost of the expenses that your professional charged you? Do the reports and statements you receive come from the same firm? Questions like these can help you get a sense of how well the reference knows their professional and whether or not they are a quality reference.

A good reference is a bit like icing on the cake. It's nice to have them, but nothing speaks louder than a good track record and quality experience. And remember that a good reference, while nice to hear, is relatively cheap. How many times have you heard someone on the golf course or at work telling you how great their stockbroker is? But how many times have you heard about the bad investments or losses they have experienced?

4. Use the Internet. As a final step before picking up the phone and calling your candidates, do some digging to discover if anyone on your list has a history of unlawful or unethical practices, or has been disciplined for any of their professional behavior or decisions. Don't worry, you don't have to hire a private investigator. You can easily find this information on the Financial Industry Regulatory Authority's (FINRA) online BrokerCheck tool: http://www.finra.org/Investors/ToolsCalculators/BrokerCheck/.

You should obviously explore the website of a potential professional and the website of the firm that they represent. The Internet allows you to go beyond the online business card of a professional to gain access to information that they don't control. It may all be good information! Or a brief search of the Internet could reveal a sketchy past. The best part is that the Internet allows you to find helpful information in an anonymous fashion.

Start with Google (www.google.com) and search the name of a potential professional and their firm. Keep your eyes trained on third party sources such as articles, blog posts or news stories that mention the professional. You can also check a professional's compliance records online with the Financial Industry Regulatory Authority (FINRA) and the Securities and Exchange Commission (SEC). If you want to dig deeper, you can combine search terms like "scams," "lawsuits," "suspensions" and "fraud" with a professional's or firm's name to see what information arises. More likely than not, you won't find anything. But if you do, you'll be glad that you checked.

HOW TO INTERVIEW CANDIDATES

After vetting your candidates and narrowing down a list of professionals that you think might be a good fit for you, it's time to start interviewing.

When you meet in person with a professional, you want to take advantage of your time with them. The presentations and information that they share with you will be important to pay attention to, but you will also want to control some aspects of the interview. After a professional has told you what they want you to hear, it's time to ask your own questions to get the specific information you need to make your decision.

Make sure to prepare a list of questions and an informal agenda so that you can keep track of what you want to ask and what points you want the professional to touch on during the interview. Using the same questions and agenda will also allow you to more easily compare the professionals after you have interviewed them all. Remember that these interviews are just that, *interviews*. You are meeting with several professionals to determine with whom you want to work. Don't agree to anything or sign anything during an interview until after you have made your final decision.

It can also be helpful to put a time limit on your interviews and to meet the professionals at their offices. The time limit will keep things on track and will allow structured time for presentations and questions/discussion. By meeting them at their office, you can get a sense of the work environment, the staff culture and attitude, and how the firm does business. If you are unable to travel to a professional's office and must meet them at your home or office, make sure that your interviews are scheduled with plenty of time between so the professionals don't cross each other's paths.

You can use the following questions during an initial interview to get an understanding of how each professional does business and whether they are a good fit for you:

1. How do you charge for your services? How much do you charge? This information should be easy to find on their website, but if you don't see it, ask. Find out if they charge an initial planning fee, if they charge a percentage for assets under their management and if they make money by selling specific financial products or services. If so, you should follow up by asking how much the service costs. This will give you an idea of how they really make their money and if they have incentive to sell certain products over others. Make sure you understand exactly how you will be charged so there are no surprises down the road if you decide to work with this person.

2. What are your credentials, licenses, and certifications? There are Certified Financial Planners (CFPs), Chartered Financial Consultants (ChFCs), Investment Advisor Representatives, Certified Public Accountants (CPAs) and Personal Financial Specialists (PFSs). Whatever their credentials or titles, you want to be sure that the professional you work with is an expert in the field relevant to your circumstances. If you want someone to manage your money, you will most likely look for an Investment Advisor. Someone that works with an independent firm will likely have a team of CPAs, CFPs and other financial experts upon whom they can draw. If you like the professional you are meeting with and you think they might be a good fit, but they don't have the accounting experience you want them to have, ask about their firm and the resources available to them. If they work closely with CPAs that are experienced in your needs, it could be a good match.

3. What are the financial services that you and your firm provide? The question within the question here is, "Can you help me achieve my goals?" Some people can only provide you with investment advice, and others are tax consultants. You will likely want to work with someone that provides a complete suite of financial planning services and products that touch on retirement planning, insurance options, legacy and estate structuring, and tax planning. Whatever services they provide, make sure they meet your needs and your anticipated needs.

4. What kinds of clients do you work with the most? A lot of financial professionals work within a niche: retirement planning, risk assessment, life insurance, etc. Finding someone who works with other people that are in the same financial boat as you and who have similar goals can be an important way to make sure they understand your needs. While someone might be a crackerjack annuities cowboy, you might not be interested in that option. Ask follow-up questions that will really help you understand where their expertise lies and whether or not their experience lines up with your needs. When it comes to choosing an estate planner, any estate planner worth his or her salt will have at least one, if not several, elder law attorneys that she regularly refers to and consults with. Planning your legacy and organizing your estate bring with their own unique set of requirements and challenges with them and you want to make sure that you choose someone who specializes in this area.

5. May I see a sample of one of your financial plans? You wouldn't buy a car without test driving it, and you should not work with a professional without seeing a sample of how they do business. While there is no formal structure that a financial plan has to follow, the variation between professionals can help you find someone who "speaks your language." One professional may provide you with an in-depth analysis that relies heavily on info graphics and diagrams. Someone else may give you a seven page review of your assets and general recommendations. By seeing a sample plan, you can narrow down who presents information in the way that you desire and in ways that you understand.

6. How do you approach investing? You may be entirely in the dark about how to approach your investments, or you might have some guiding principles. Either way, ask each candidate what their philosophy is. Some will resonate with you and some won't. A good professional who has a realistic approach to investing won't promise you the moon or tell you that they can make you a lot of money. Professionals who are successful at retirement planning and full service financial management will tell you that they will listen to your goals, risk tolerance and comfort level with different types of investment strategies. Working with someone that you trust is critical, and this question in particular can help you find out who you can and who you can't.

7. How do you remain in contact with your clients? Does your prospective professional hold annual, quarterly or monthly meetings? How often do *you* want to meet with your professional? Some people want to check in once a year, go over everything and make sure their ducks are all in a row. If any changes over the previous year or additions to their legacy planning strategy came up, they'll do it on that date. Other people want a monthly update to be more involved in the decision making process and to understand what's happening with their portfolio. You basically need to determine the right degree of involvement for both you and your financial professional. You'll also want to feel out how your professional communicates. Do you prefer phone calls or face-to-face meetings? Do you want your professional to explain things to you in detail or to summarize for you what decisions they've made? Is the professional willing to give you their direct phone number or their email address? More importantly, do you want that information and do you want to be able to contact them in those ways?

8. Are you my main contact, or do you work with a team? This is another way of finding out how involved with you your professional will be, and how often they will meet with you. It is also a way to discover how the firm they represent operates and manages their clients. Some professionals will answer their own phone, meet with you regularly and have your home phone number on speed dial. Others will meet with you once a year and have a partner or assistant check in with you every quarter to give you an update. Other companies take an entirely team-based approach whereby clients have a main contact but their portfolio is handled by a team of professionals that represent the firm. One way isn't better than another, but one way will be best for you. Find out how the professional you are interviewing operates before entering into an agreement.

9. How do you provide a unique experience for your clients? This is a polite way of asking, "Why should I work with you?" A professional should have a compelling answer to this question that connects with you. Their answer will likely touch on their investment philosophy, their communication style and their expertise. If you hear them describing strengths and philosophies that resonate with you, keep them on your list. Some professionals will tell you that they will make investments with your money that match your values, others will say they will maximize your returns and others will say they will protect your capital while structuring your assets for income. Whatever you're looking for in a professional, you will most likely find it in the answer to this question.

This last question you will want to ask *yourself* after you've met with someone who you are considering hiring:

10. Did they ask questions and show signs that they were interested in working with me? A professional who will structure your assets to reflect your risk tolerance and to position you for a comfortable retirement must be a good listener. You will want to pass by a professional who talks non-stop and tells you what to do without listening to what you want them to do. If you felt they listened well and understood your needs, and seemed interested and experienced in your situation, then they might be right for you.

THE IMPORTANCE OF INDEPENDENCE

Not all investment firms and financial professionals are created equal. The information in this book has systematically shown that leveraging investments for income and accumulation in today's market requires new ideas and modern planning. In short, you need innovative ideas to come up with the creative solutions that will provide you with the retirement that you want. Innovation thrives on independence. No matter how good a financial professional is, the firm that they represent needs to operate on principles that make sense in today's economy. Remember, advice about money has been around forever. Good advice, however, changes with the times.

Timing the market, relying on the sale of stocks for income and banking on high treasury and bond returns are not strategies. They aren't even realistic ways to make money or to generate income. Working with an independent agent can help you break free from the old ways of thinking and position you to create a realistic retirement plan.

Working with an independent professional who relies on fee-based income tied to the success of their performance will also give you greater peace of mind. When you do well, they do well, and that's the way it should be. Your independent financial professional will make sure that:

- Your assets are organized and structured to reflect your risk tolerance.
- Your assets will be available to you when you need them and in the way that you need them.
- You will have a lifetime income that will support your lifestyle through your retirement.
- You are handling your taxes as efficiently as possible.
- Your legacy is in order.
- Your Red Money is turned into Yellow Money, and is managed in your best interest.

» *Remember Alex and Lizzie from Chapter 1? Even though they knew they had Social Security benefits coming, they placed some money in savings and each had a pension or a 401(k).* **Before they met with a financial professional, they had no idea what their retirement would look like.** *After they met with an agent, they knew exactly what types of assets they had, how much they were worth, how much risk they were exposed to and how they were going to be distributed. They also created an income plan so that they could pay their bills every month the moment they retired, and they maximized their Social Security benefit by targeting the year and month they would get the most lifetime benefits. After their income needs were met, they were able to continue accumulating wealth by investing their extra assets to serve them in the future and contribute to their legacy. Their professional also helped them make decisions that impacted their taxes, protecting the value of their assets and allowing them to keep more of their money.*

*This isn't a fairy tale scenario. This is an example of how much you stand to gain by meeting with a financial professional who can help you create a planful approach to your retirement. The concept of Know So and Hope So didn't just apply to their money, it also applied to Alex and Lizzie. They **hoped** that they would have enough for retirement and that they had worked hard enough and saved enough to maintain their lifestyle. Working with a financial professional allowed them to **know** that their income needs were secured and structured to provide them with income for the rest of their lives and with some money to spare. What's more, they got the rest of their affairs in order so they could rest assured that their children would be well-cared for and that the transferring of their assets to their beneficiaries would be as seamless as possible.*

Now, ask yourself: Is your retirement built on hopes and dreams, or a solid, predictable plan?

IT'S WORTH IT!

Finding, interviewing and selecting a financial professional can seem like a daunting task. And honestly, it will take a good amount of work to narrow the field and find the one you want. In the end, it is worth the blood, sweat and tears. Your retirement, lifestyle, assets and legacy are all on the line. The choices you make today will have lasting impacts on your life and the life of your loved ones. Working with someone you trust and know you can rely on to make decisions that will benefit you is invaluable. The work it takes to find them is something you will never regret.

Here is a recap of why working with a financial professional is the best financial decision you can make:

CHAPTER 13 RECAP //

- If you feel you have more *Hope So* than *Know So* about your money and what your retirement is going to look like, working with a financial professional will give you clarity and confidence about what decisions are best for you.

- It is difficult for individual investors to not make emotional decisions about their investments. Financial professionals work with your risk tolerance, income needs and assets to find the most logical, efficient and beneficial way for you to structure your investments.

- As the DALBAR report showed, a majority of individual investors sell low when the market goes down and buy high when it goes back up. This is literally the exact opposite of what they should do to maximize their returns. Why? Emotions.

- A financial professional can help you change strategies when the market isn't going your way, but they won't abandon ship. They will stick to a planful approach. Your retirement isn't based on individual products or investments. It is based on a well-planned strategy that your financial professional is qualified to provide.

- Yellow Money is different from a mutual fund or a 401(k) because, while funds and 401(k)s are investment tools, they are not investment strategies. A 401(k) can be particularly misconceiving because your employer isn't truly structuring your investments inside the 401(k). They are simply providing you with a few options. The same goes for mutual funds. They are not truly managed by someone who is obligated to have your best interests and your risk tolerance in mind. In fact, the investment strategies of mutual funds change on a regular basis, and you might not know about it until you get an annual report a *month* later.

- The biggest difference between working with a financial professional to manage your funds, and buying a mutual fund is that, while a mutual fund buys 20 stocks and pegs its earnings on the overall performance of the portfolio, a financial professional works with you to create an overall financial strategy that meets your needs. It may or may not include mutual funds.

- As an individual investor, do you really have an overarching strategy for your financial portfolio? How did you come up with your selections? Do you know how they are individually managed? Do you know how to make changes to your portfolio that reflect your risk tolerance? Do you know what your risk tolerance is?

- Managed money has a specific criteria and a professional will fit that into your overall financial plan so that it works the way you want it to.

- Not all investment firms and financial professionals are created equal. Working with an independent professional will give you more options that are customizable to your life.

Glossary

ANNUAL RESET *(ANNUAL RATCHET, CLIQUET)* – Crediting methods measuring index movement over a one year period. Positive interest is calculated and credited at the end of each contract year and cannot be lost if the index subsequently declines. Say that the index increased from 100 to 110 in one year and the indexed annuity had an 80 percent participation rate. The insurance company would take the 10 percent gross index gain for the year (110-100/100), apply the participation rate (10 percent index gain x 80 percent rate) and credit 8 percent interest to the annuity. But, what if in the following year the index declined back to 100? The individual would keep the 8 percent interest earned and simply receive zero interest for the down year. An annual reset structure preserves credited gains and treats negative index periods as years with zero growth.

ANNUITANT – The person, usually the annuity owner, whose life expectancy is used to calculate the income payment amount on the annuity.

ANNUITY – An annuity is a contract issued by an insurance company that often serves as a type of savings plan used by individuals looking for long term growth and protection of assets that will likely be needed within retirement.

AVERAGING – Index values may either be measured from a start point to an end point (point-to-point) or values between the start point and end point may be averaged to determine an ending value. Index values may be averaged over the days, weeks, months or quarters of the period.

BENEFICIARY – A beneficiary is the person designated to receive payments due upon the death of the annuity owner or the annuitant themselves.

BONUS RATE – A bonus rate is the "extra" or "additional" interest paid during the first year (the initial guarantee period), typically used as an added incentive to get consumers to select their annuity policy over another.

CALL OPTION *(ALSO SEE PUT OPTION)* – Gives the holder the right to buy an underlying security or index at a specified price on or before a given date.

CAP – The maximum interest rate that will be credited to the annuity for the year or period. The cap usually refers to the maximum interest credited after applying the participation rate or yield spread. If the index methodology showed a 20 percent increase, the participation rate was 60 percent and the maximum interest cap was 10 percent, the contract would credit 10 percent interest. A few annuities use a maximum gain cap instead of a maximum interest cap with the participation rate or yield spread applied to the lesser of the gain or the cap. If the index methodology showed a 20 percent increase, the participation rate was 60 percent and the maximum gain cap was 10 percent, the contract would credit 6 percent interest.

COMPOUND INTEREST – Interest is earned on both the original principal and on previously earned interest. It is more favorable than simple interest. Suppose that your original principal was $1 and your interest rate was 10 percent for five years. With simple interest, your value is ($1 + $0.10 interest each year) = $1.50. With compound interest, your value is ($1 x 1.10 x 1.10 x 1.10 x 1.10 x 1.10) = $1.61. The advantage of compound interest over simple interest becomes greater as each subsequent period passes.

CREDITING METHOD *(ALSO SEE METHODOLOGY)* – The formula(s) used to determine the excess interest that is credited above the minimum interest guarantee.

DEATH BENEFITS – The payment the annuity owner's estate or beneficiaries will receive if he or she dies before the annuity matures. On most annuities, this is equal to the current account value. Some annuities offer an enhanced value at death via an optional rider that has a monthly or annual fee associated with it.

EXCESS INTEREST – Interest credited to the annuity contract above the minimum guaranteed interest rate. In an indexed annuity the excess interest is determined by applying a stated crediting method to a specific index or indices.

FIXED ANNUITY – A contract issued by an insurance company guaranteeing a minimum interest rate with the crediting of excess interest determined by the performance of the insurer's general account. Index annuities are fixed annuities.

FIXED DEFERRED ANNUITY – With fixed annuities, an insurance company offers a guaranteed interest rate plus safety of your principal and earnings ((subject to the claims-paying ability of the insurance company). Your interest rate will be reset periodically, based on economic and other factors, but is guaranteed to never fall below a certain rate.

FREE WITHDRAWALS – Withdrawals that are free of surrender charges.

INDEX – The underlying external benchmark upon which the crediting of excess interest is based, also a measure of the prices of a group of securities.

IRA *(INDIVIDUAL RETIREMENT ACCOUNT)* – An IRA is a tax-advantaged personal savings plan that lets an individual set aside money for retirement. All or part of the participant's contributions may be tax deductible, depending on the type of IRA chosen and the participant's personal financial circumstances. Distributions from many employer-sponsored retirement plans may be eligible to be rolled into an IRA to continue tax-deferred growth until the funds are needed. An annuity can be used as an IRA; that is, IRA funds can be used to purchase an annuity.

IRA ROLLOVER – IRA rollover is the phrase used when an individual who has a balance in an employer-sponsored retirement plan transfers that balance into an IRA. Such an exchange, when properly handled, is a tax-advantaged transaction.

LIQUIDITY – The ease with which an asset is convertible to cash. An asset with high liquidity provides flexibility, in that the owner can easily convert it to cash at any time, but it also tends to decrease profitability.

MARKET RISK – The risk of the market value of an asset fluctuating up or down over time. In a fixed or fixed indexed annuity, the original principal and credited interest are not subject to market risk. Even if the index declines, the annuity owner would receive no less than their original principal back if they decided to cash in the policy at the end of the surrender period. Unlike a security, indexed annuities guarantee the original premium and the premium is backed by, and is as safe as, the insurance company that issued it (subject to the claims-paying ability of the insurance company).

METHODOLOGY *(ALSO SEE CREDITING METHOD)* – The way that interest crediting is calculated. On fixed indexed annuities, there are a variety of different methods used to determine how index movement becomes interest credited.

MINIMUM GUARANTEED RETURN *(MINIMUM INTEREST RATE)* – Fixed indexed annuities typically provide a minimum guaranteed return over the life of the contract. At the time that the owner chooses to terminate the contract, the cash surrender value is compared to a second value calculated using the minimum guaranteed return and the higher of the two values is paid to the annuity owner.

OPTION – A contract which conveys to its holder the right, but not the obligation, to buy or sell something at a specified price on or before a given date. After this given date the option ceases to exist. Insurers typically buy options to provide for the excess interest potential. Options may be American style whereby they may be exercised at any time prior to the given date, or they may have to be exercised only during a specified window. Options that may only be exercised during a specified period are European-style options.

OPTION RISK – Most insurers create the potential for excess interest in an indexed annuity by buying options. Say that you could buy a share of stock for $50. If you bought the stock and it rose to $60 you could sell it and net a $10 profit. But, if the stock price fell to $40 you'd have a $10 loss. Instead of buying the actual stock, we could buy an option that gave us the right to buy the stock for $50 at any time over the next year. The cost of the option is $2. If the stock price rose to $60 we would exercise our option, buy the stock at $50 and make $10 (less the $2 cost of the option). If the price of the stock fell to $40, $30 or $10, we wouldn't use the option and it would expire. The loss is limited to $2 – the cost of the option.

PARTICIPATION RATE – The percentage of positive index movement credited to the annuity. If the index methodology determined that the index increased 10 percent and the indexed annuity participated in 60 percent of the increase, it would be said that the contract has a 60 percent participation rate. Participation rates may also be expressed as asset fees or yield spreads.

POINT-TO-POINT – A crediting method measuring index move-ment from an absolute initial point to the absolute end point for a period. An index had a period starting value of 100 and a period ending value of 120. A point-to-point method would record a positive index movement of 20 [120-100] or a 20 percent positive movement [(120-100)/100]. Point-to-point usually refers to an-nual periods; however the phrase is also used instead of term end point to refer to multiple year periods.

PREMIUM BONUS – A premium bonus is additional money that is credited to the accumulation account of an annuity policy under certain conditions.

PUT OPTION *(ALSO SEE CALL OPTION)* – Gives the holder the right to sell an underlying security or index at a specified price on or before a given date.

QUALIFIED ANNUITIES *(QUALIFIED MONEY)* – Qualified annuities are annuities purchased for funding an IRA, 403(b) tax-deferred annuity or other type of retirement arrangements. An IRA or qualified retirement plan provides the tax deferral. An annuity contract should be used to fund an IRA or qualified retirement plan to benefit from an annuity's features other than tax deferral, including the safety features, lifetime income payout option and death benefit protection.

REQUIRED MINIMUM DISTRIBUTION *(RMD)* – The amount of money that Traditional, SEP and SIMPLE IRA owners and qualified plan participants must begin distributing from their retirement accounts by April 1 following the year they reach age 70.5. RMD amounts must then be distributed each subsequent year.

RETURN FLOOR – Another way of saying minimum guaranteed return.

ROTH IRA – Like other IRA accounts, the Roth IRA is simply a holding account that manages your stocks, bonds, annuities, mutual funds and CD's. However, future withdrawals (including earnings and interest) are typically tax-advantaged once the account has been open for five years and the account holder is age 59.5.

RULE OF 72 – Tells you approximately how many years it takes a sum to double at a given rate. It's handy to be able to figure out, without using a calculator, that when you're earning a 6 percent return, for example, by dividing 6 percent into 72, you'll find that it takes 12 years for money to double. Conversely, if you know it took a sum twelve years to double you could divide 12 into 72 to determine the annual return (6 percent).

SIMPLE INTEREST *(ALSO SEE COMPOUND INTEREST)* – Interest is only earned on the principal balance.

SPLIT ANNUITY – A split annuity is the term given to an effective strategy that utilizes two or more different annuity products – one designed to generate monthly income and the other to restore the original starting principal over a set period of time.

STANDARD & POOR'S 500 *(S&P 500)* – The most widely used external index by fixed indexed annuities. Its objective is to be a benchmark to measure and report overall U.S. stock market performance. It includes a representative sample of 500 common stocks from companies trading on the New York Stock Exchange, American Stock Exchange, and NASDAQ National Market System. The index represents the price or market value of the underlying stocks and does not include the value of reinvested dividends of the underlying stocks.

STOCK MARKET INDEX – A report created from a type of statistical measurement that shows up or down changes in a specific financial market, usually expressed as points and as a percentage, in a number of related markets, or in an economy as a whole (i.e. S&P 500 or New York Stock Exchange).

SURRENDER CHARGE – A charge imposed for withdrawing funds or terminating an annuity contract prematurely. There is no industry standard for surrender charges, that is, each annuity product has its own unique surrender charge schedule. The charge is usually expressed as a percentage of the amount withdrawn prematurely from the contract. The percentage tends to decline over time, ultimately becoming zero.

TRADITIONAL IRA – See IRA (Individual Retirement Account)

TERM END POINT – Crediting methods measuring index movements over a greater timeframe than a year or two. The opposite of an annual reset method. Also referred to as a term point-to-point method. Say that the index value was at 100 on the first day of the period. If the calculated index value was at 150 at the end of the period the positive index movement would be 50 percent (150-100/100). The company would credit a percentage of this movement as excess interest. Index movement is calculated and interest credited at the end of the term and interim movements during the period are ignored.

TERM HIGH POINT (HIGH WATER MARK) – A type of term end point structure that uses the highest anniversary index level as the end point. Say that the index value was at 100 on the first day of the period, reached a value of 160 at the end of a contract year during the period, and ended the period at 150. A term high point method would use the 160 value – the highest contract anniversary point reached during the period, as the end point and the gross index gain would be 60 percent (160-100/100). The company would then apply a participation rate to the gain.

TERM YIELD SPREAD – A type of term end point structure which calculates the total index gain for a period, computes the annual compound rate of return deducts a yield spread from the annual rate of return and then recalculates the total index gain for the period based on the net annual rate. Say that an index increased from 100 to 200 by the end of a nine year period. This is the equivalent of an 8 percent compound annual interest rate. If the annuity had a 2 percent term yield spread this would be deducted from the annual interest rate (8 percent-2 percent) and the net rate would be credited to the contract (6 percent) for each of the nine years. Total index gain may also be computed by using the highest anniversary index level as the end point.

VARIABLE ANNUITY – A contract issued by an insurance company offering separate accounts invested in a wide variety of stocks and/or bonds. The investment risk is borne by the annuity owner. Variable annuities are considered securities and require appropriate securities registration.

1035 EXCHANGE – The 1035 exchange refers to the section of tax code that allows annuity owners the flexibility to exchange one annuity for another without incurring any immediate tax liabilities. This action is most often utilized when an annuity holder decides they want to upgrade an annuity to a more favorable one, but they do not want to activate unnecessary tax liabilities that would typically be encountered when surrendering an existing annuity contract.

401(K) ROLLOVER – See <u>IRA Rollover</u>